MW01285950

The North Korean People's Army

**ORDER OF THE KOREAN PEOPLE'S ARMY FOUNDATION
COMMEMORATION (Chosŏn Inmin'gun Ch'anggŭn Kinyŏm Hunjang)**

Established 25 January 1968

Worn on the left chest, it is awarded to soldiers of the (North) Korean People's Army and Security Forces for support of military policies of the Korean Labor Party. The base of the award is a pentagon of 65 mm long golden rays. On top of the pentagon is a five-point red star that is 60 mm in diameter. Inside the star is a 2.5 mm wide golden ring that is 32 mm in diameter. In the ring is a golden national emblem that is 27 mm high and 22.5 mm wide, which is fastened to a white plate. On the obverse is written *Chosŏn Inmin'gun Ch'anggŏn Kinyŏm Hunjang*; the issue number; 1968.2.8; and a screw back. Source: *Nodong Sinmun* (P'yŏngyang) 1 February 1968. (Art by Matthew S. Minnich)

The North Korean People's Army

ORIGINS AND CURRENT TACTICS

JAMES M. MINNICH

Naval Institute Press
ANNAPOLIS, MARYLAND

Naval Institute Press
291 Wood Road
Annapolis, MD 21402

Naval Institute Press

Library of Congress Cataloging-in-Publication Data
Minnich, James M.
The North Korean People's Army : origins and current tactics /
James M. Minnich.
p.   cm.
Includes bibliographical references and index.
ISBN 1-59114-525-2 (alk. paper)
1. Korea (North). Chosæon Inmin'gun. I. Title.
UA853.K5654   2005
355'.0095193—dc22

2005021005

Printed in the United States of America on acid-free paper

25 24 23 22 21 20 19 18   9 8 7 6 5 4 3

Dedicated to the memory of my father, Mervel A. Minnich Jr.;
to my mother, Charlene Minnich; to my loving wife, Yong S.;
and to my adult children, David Robert and Wayne Thomas

Contents

List of Illustrations

TABLES

Preface

For more than fifty years, the combined armed forces of the United States and the Republic of Korea have courageously shed sweat and blood in their tireless deterrence of the world's third largest army—the North Korean People's Army (NKPA). Despite this half century stand-off, along the world's most militarized stretch of land known as the demilitarized zone, much remains unknown about this ruthless foe. James M. Minnich masterfully blends academic knowledge with nearly twenty-five years of military experience to explain the NKPA's origins, military ideology, strategy, combat formations, and tactics to ensure that no coalition combatant has to fight the NKPA without a full understanding of this ruthless, reclusive belligerent.

At the outset, Minnich examines the initial, crucial years of the formation of the North Korean state and its army. Inaugurated in February 1948, the NKPA burgeoned from the experiences of its partisan roots, from direct Soviet tutelage, and from Chinese Communist influences. Solidly grounded in primary sources and buttressed by the judicial use of secondary sources, Minnich traces the forging elements of these three groups—Korean partisans, the Soviet Army, and Chinese Communists upon the NKPA. Each group uniquely contributed to the cauldron that

forged the leadership, combat formations, combat equipment, and training that prepared an army to mount a surprise attack that triggered the
first shooting conflict of the Cold War; the forgotten war that nearly
ignited World War III.

Later, Minnich draws the parallel between the original three influences on the NKPA and its current military ideology, strategy, combat
formations, and tactics. For over fifty years the NKPA has dramatically
increased in size and capability, yet remains true to its initial precepts.
Drawing heavily upon military education at the Republic of Korea
Army College, Minnich conducts a detailed examination of the NKPA's
current military tactics, including its seven forms of offensive maneuver,
two forms of defense, and tactical artillery groupings tactics. This book
is a must-read for students of Korean history and those seeking a deeper
understanding of the NKPA, but unequivocally it is required reading for
every one of the 600,000 United States soldiers, sailors, airmen, marines,
and military planners who must remain prepared to rapidly deploy to
Korea then close with and destroy this most dangerous of enemies.

Acknowledgments

I am indebted to many people for their unique contributions to this study, including several professors who have not only educated me but have also inspired me. First, it is appropriate to recognize my Harvard University thesis advisor—Professor Carter J. Eckert—for suggesting this topic, providing me with an initial orientation, and for critiquing this work throughout the writing process. Likewise, there are many others who have aided my thinking, including Professors Graham T. Allison, Daniel Botsman, Carter J. Eckert, Sun Joo Kim, Sung-Yoon Lee, Robert Paarlberg, Ezra F. Vogel, Alan M. Wachman, and Dr. John P. White.

A special note of gratitude is accorded to the Harvard-Yenching Library staff, with particular mention of Choong Nam Yoon, librarian for the Korean Collection.

Finally, during my studies at the Republic of Korea Army College in 2001, I was taught and assisted by many fine Korean officers, whom I will long remember. Included in this group of professionals are Lt. Col. Kim Yong-bŏm (my faculty sponsor and North Korea military tactics instructor) and Lt. Col. Kim Hŭng-t'aek (my student sponsor and dear friend).

Abbreviations and Acronyms

1TE   First Tactical Echelon
2TE   Second Tactical Echelon
ADA   Air Defense Artillery
AO   Area of Operation
AP   Antipersonnel
AT   Antitank
BC   Border Constabulary (*kyŏngbitae*)
Bde   Brigade
Bn   Battalion
Btry   Battery
C2   Command and Control
CAG   Corps Artillery Group
Co   Company
CCF   Chinese Communist Forces
CCP   Chinese Communist Party
CPKI   Committee for the Preparation of Korean Independence
         (*Chosŏn Kŏn'guk Chunbi Wiwŏnhoe*)
DAG   Division Artillery Group
Div   Division

DPRK   Democratic People's Republic of Korea
FNKPAB   Five North Korean Provinces' Administrative Bureau
            (*Pukchosŏn Odo Haengjŏngguk*)
FRA   Fatherland Restoration Association
            (*Choguk Kwangbokhoe*)
GMD   Guomindang (or Kuomintang; the Nationalist Party)
Inf   Infantry
km   Kilometer
KNRP   Korean National Revolutionary Party
KPRA   Korean People's Revolutionary Army (*Chosŏn Inmin Hyŏgmyŏnggun*)
KVA   Korean Volunteer Army (*Chosŏn Ŭiyonggun*)
LOA   Limit of Advance
Loc   Location
LST   Landing ship tank
mm   Millimeter
MND   Ministry of National Defense (*Powisŏng*)
MRL   Multiple Rocket Launcher
NCKIL   North China Korean Independence League
            (*Hwapuk Chosŏn Tongnip Tongmaeng*)
NCKYF   North China Korean Youth Federation
NEAJUA   Northeast Anti-Japanese United Army
NKIPC   North Korean Interim People's Committee
NKPA   (North) Korean People's Army (*Chosŏn Inmin'gun*)
NKPC   North Korean People's Committee
NKWP   North Korean Workers' Party (*Pukchosŏn Nodongdang*)
PLA   People's Liberation Army
Plt   Platoon
RAG   Regimental Artillery Group
Regt   Regiment
RMTU   Reserve Military Training Unit
ROK   Republic of Korea
ROKA   Republic of Korea Army
RPG   Rocket-propelled Grenade
SCGTC   Security Cadre General Training Center
            (*Poan Kanbu Ch'ong Hullyŏnso*)

SOF	Special Operation Forces
SP	Self-propelled
UNTCOK	United Nations Temporary Commission on Korea
Wpn	Weapon
YHD	Yi Hong-gwang Detachment (*Yi Hong-gwang Chidae*)

Personalities

An Kil (1907–1947): *Kapsanist;* Manchurian-based partisan leader during the early 1930s; member of the First Route Army of the Northeast Anti-Japanese United Army (NEAJUA); battalion political commissar of the Soviet 88th Special Brigade (1941–1946); and Security Cadre General Training Center (SCGTC) chief of staff (later renamed the People's Army Group) (1946–1947); died of illness in December 1947.

Chistiakov, Ivan Mikhailovich: Soviet; colonel general and Twenty-fifth Army commander from the summer of 1945 until April 1947.

Cho Man-sik: Native Korean and staunch anti-Japanese nationalist leader who was born in Kangsŏ County, South P'yŏngan Province. Later he served as chairman of the Five North Korean Provinces' Administrative Bureau (FNKPAB) from 8 October 1945 until his arrest in January 1946.

Ch'oe Hyŏn (1907–?): *Kapsanist;* Manchurian-based partisan leader during the early 1930s; 4th Division commander of the Second Army of the First Route Army of the NEAJUA (1936–1941); company commander of the Soviet 88th Special Brigade (1941–1945); Kanggye Detachment commander; Ministry of National Defense Political Bureau officer; 2nd (North) Korean People's Army (NKPA) Division commander during the Korean War; and post-war National Defense minister.

Ch'oe Yong-gŏn (1900–1976): *Kapsanist;* born in North P'yŏngan Province, as a youth, he was formally educated by Cho Man-sik; joined March First Movement (1919); Wun'an Military Academy graduate (1925); military science instructor at Huangpu (Whampoa) Military Academy; Manchurian-based partisan leader (from 1926); political commissar of the Seventh Army of the Second Route Army of the NEAJUA (1936–1941); Soviet 88th Special Brigade political commissar (1941–1945); FNKPAB Security Bureau chief (1945–1946); North Korean Interim People's Committee (NKIPC) Security Bureau chief (1946); Central Security Cadre School commandant (1946–1947); SCGTC commander (1946–1947); People's Assembly of North Korea, standing vice chairman (1947–1948); (North) Korean People's Army commander (1948); National Defense minister from September 1948; Presidium deputy chairman of the Supreme People's Congress (1956); Presidium chairman of the Supreme People's Congress (1957); member of the Politburo Presidium of the NKWP (from 1966); member of the Secretariat of the NKWP (from 1970); and titular head of state (1963–1972).

Kang Kŏn (1918–1950): *Kapsanist;* born in Sangju County, North Kyŏngsang Province; subordinate commander in the Third Route Army of the NEAJUA; battalion commander of the Soviet 88th Special Brigade (1941–1945); 2nd NKPA Division commander (1946); NKPA chief of staff (1948–1950); and Front chief of staff during the Korean War; killed near Andong, China, by a land mine explosion on 8 September 1950.

Kim Ch'aek (1903–1951): *Kapsanist;* born in North Hamgyŏng Province; Manchurian-based partisan leader during the early 1930s; political commissar of the Third Army of the Third Route Army of the NEAJUA (1936–1941); battalion political commissar of the Soviet 88th Special Brigade (1941–1945); P'yŏngyang Institute commandant

(1945–1947); SCGTC deputy commander (1946–1947); North Korean People's Committee (NKPC) vice chairman (1947–1948); National Defense Bureau chief (1948); DPRK vice premier (1948–1951); and Front commander during the Korean War, from September 1950 until killed in action in January 1951.

Kim Il (?–1985): *Kapsanist;* politics and economic major of the University of Tashkent, USSR; company commander of the Soviet 88th Special Brigade; 1st NKPA Division cultural commander; Defense Ministry cultural commander; member of the Politburo Presidium of the NKWP (from 1966); deputy premier; member of the Secretariat of the NKWP (from 1970); and DPRK vice president before his death in 1985.

Kim Il Sung (Kim Il-sŏng, 1912–1994): *Kapsanist;* born Kim Sŏng-ju near P'yŏngyang; Manchurian-based partisan leader during the early 1930s; 6th Division commander of the First Route Army of the NEAJUA (1936–1941); battalion commander of the Soviet 88th Special Brigade (1941–1945); P'yŏngyang *Komendatura* deputy commander; NKIPC chairman; member of the Politburo Presidium of the NKWP (from 1966); member of the Secretariat of the NKWP (from 1970); and DPRK premier/president from 1948 until his death on 8 July 1994.

Kim Kwang-hyŏp (1915–?): *Kapsanist;* company commander of the Soviet 88th Special Brigade; 3rd NKPA Division commander; II NKPA Corps commander; post-war national Defense minister; and member of the Politburo Presidium of the NKWP (from 1966).

(Kim) Mu Chŏng (1904–1951?): *Yananist;* born in Kyŏngsŏng County, North Hamgyŏng Province; went to China (1922); graduate of the Henan Military Academy of the Chinese Nationalist Army; artillery lieutenant during Northern Expedition; Chinese Communist Party (CCP) member (1926); Chinese Communist Eighth Route Army leader; Yanan-based Korean Volunteer Army commander; SCGTC artillery commander; NKWP Central Committee member (1948); and II NKPA Corps commander (from 1950); purged in December 1950 and returned to China.

Kim Tu-bong (1889–1961?): *Yananist;* born in Korea, he moved to China in 1919; North China Korean Independence League (NCKIL) chairman in Yanan, China (1942); NKIPC vice chairman; returned to Korea (1945); New People's Party chairman; standing chairman of the presidium of the Supreme People's Assembly from its inception in February 1947 until he was purged from the government in 1957.

Kim Ŭng (1928–?): *Yananist;* Huangpu (Whampoa) Military Academy graduate; fled to Yanan, China (1930s); (brigade or division) commander in the Chinese Communist Eighth Route Army during Chinese civil war; 1st NKPA Division commander; I NKPA Corps commander (1950); Front chief of staff after death of Kang Kŏn (September 1950); Front commander (1953); vice minister of National Defense (1954?); purged in 1958; and ambassador to Yemen (1973–1978).

Korotkov, Gennadii Petrovich: Soviet; lieutenant general and commander of the Twenty-fifth Army from April 1947.

Lebedev, Nikolai Georgievich: Soviet; major general and member of the Military Council of the Twenty-fifth Army (1941–1947); chief of the Soviet Civil Administration in North Korea (autumn 1947–December 1948).

Meretskov, Kirill Afanasievich (1897–1985): Soviet; marshal and commander of the Soviet Maritime Army Group, renamed the First Far Eastern Front in August 1945, renamed the Maritime Military District in September 1945. This unit, under the command of Marshal Meretskov, was the higher headquarters for the Twenty-fifth Army.

Pak Il-u (1911–?): *Yananist;* Yanan-based Korean military-political school deputy commandant; NKPC Internal Affairs Bureau chief; and DPRK Internal Affairs minister.

Pak Kŭm-chŏl (1912–?): *Kapsanist;* co-organizer of the Kapsan Operation Committee and Fatherland Restoration Association (FRA) member;

unit officer in the 1st NKPA; member of the Politburo Presidium of the NKWP (from 1966).

Pang Ho-san: *Yananist;* Huangpu (Whampoa) Military Academy graduate; Chinese Communist Party member; Yanan Military School instructor (then known as Yi Ch'un-bok); Yi Hong-gwang Detachment (YHD) combatant; 166th PLA Division commander; 6th NKPA Division commander.

Pen'kovsky, V. A.: Soviet; lieutenant general and chief of staff of the Soviet Twenty-fifth Army.

Romanenko, Andrei Alekseevich: Soviet; major general and chief of staff of the Soviet Civil Administration in North Korea (October 1945– autumn 1947); concurrently served as the Twenty-fifth Army deputy commander.

Yang Jingyu (Yang Ching-yü, ?–1940): Chinese Communist who organized the Thirty-second Red Army in Panshi County, Manchuria, in 1932. Organized and commanded the NEAJUA in 1936 until his death in February 1940.

Yi Hong-gwang (1910–1935): Korean; born in Yongin-gun, Kyŏnggido, Korea; who in 1926 moved from Korea to Manchuria, where he fought valiantly among the Chinese Communist guerrillas; close comrade in arms of Yang Jingyu; 1st NEAJUA Division commander (1935); First Army political commissar until his death in 1935; posthumously, the Yi Hong-gwang Detachment was named after him.

The North Korean
People's Army

FATHERLAND LIBERATION WAR COMMEMORATION MEDAL
(Chokuk Haebang Chŏnjaeng Kinyŏm Metal)
Established 13 August 1953

Awarded for bravery, the ribbon of the Fatherland Liberation War Commemoration Medal has five stripes, alternating red, yellow, blue, yellow, and red. The medal is a 37-mm-diameter silver disk with two jets in the sky, a tank with the number 105 in the background, and two soldiers in the foreground (one holding a machine gun and the other a North Korean flag). On the obverse is written *Widaehan Chokuk Haebang Chŏnjaeng ŭl Kinyŏmhayŏ* (For the Commemoration of the Great Fatherland Liberation War). (Art by Matthew S. Minnich)

Introduction

IN A SPEECH on 8 February 1948, Kim Il-sŏng (hereafter referred to as Kim Il Sung) augured "the inauguration of the Democratic People's Republic of Korea" and "proclaim[ed] the foundation of the (North) Korean People's Army (NKPA) [*Chosŏn Inmin'gun*]," declaring the NKPA to be "the people's first armed forces in the history of Korea."[1] In the body of his speech, Kim praised the Korean patriots of the former anti-Japanese partisan units, declaring that those groups formed the backbone of this new army. Continuing, Kim Il Sung stated: "Our People's Army is founded today as the regular army of a democratic Korea; it is, in reality, an army whose historical roots date far back; it is a glorious army inheriting the revolutionary traditions of the anti-Japanese guerrilla war, the valuable fighting experience gained, and the indomitable patriotic spirit displayed in it."[2]

Apparently, Kim Il Sung's Armed Forces Foundation Day speech was interpreted with a fair amount of ambiguity, prompting such questions as:* Is the NKPA really the people's first military? Which

---

* On the ten-year anniversary of the NKPA, Kim Il Sung refuted claims that the NKPA originated from any organization other than the Anti-Japanese Guerrilla Army. He specifically denounced several former partisan units and their leaders, including the KVA, NCKIL, and Kım Ǔl-gyu's peasant organizations, which operated near Kilju and Myongchon; referring to these men as anti-party factionalists.

anti-Japanese partisan group does the army trace its roots back through? What is the origin of that particular guerrilla element, and who were its founding leaders?[3] Over the ensuing decades, Kim Il Sung and the Central Committee of the Korean Workers' Party invested great effort to explicate such questions, and for what purposes? Overwhelmingly, the single most important reason appears to be the deification of Kim Il Sung. To this end, North Korean historiographers have woven together fact and fiction to depict the Korean revolutionary struggle as a single event that began and ended with Kim Il Sung—the sole leader who organized the partisan forces that assisted in Korea's liberation. Before Korea was liberated from Japan in 1945, Koreans throughout the peninsula lauded the exploits of the anti-Japanese partisans. However, since most of the guerrilla fighters returned to North Korea after liberation, South Korea predominately abandoned this partisan history, while North Korea embraced it—choosing to trace its national history through it (see appendix A).

Clearly, Kim Il Sung's guerrilla army was not the only Korean partisan group that existed during Japan's thirty-five-year occupation of Korea, but in Kim Il Sung's North Korea it is considered the most important group. The partisans from this group are often referred to collectively as the *Kapsan* Partisans, named after a mountain range near the Korean-Manchurian border where the group conducted some of its activities. The stories and exploits of Korea's anti-Japanese armies are interesting enough, but of greater importance might possibly be the fact that these partisan units served as schoolmasters for many of North Korea's early political and military leaders.

There are adequate sources to substantiate the existence and feats of Korean anti-Japanese partisan units; however, with few exceptions, North Korean literature, in its aggrandizement of Kim Il Sung, purposefully omits any mention that these forces operated subordinate to either the Chinese-centric, Northeast Anti-Japanese United Army (NEAJUA) in Manchuria or to the Soviet army in the Soviet Far East. Consequently, when evaluating North Korean literary sources, one is required to interpolate the data, thus, propagating inaccuracies. As a result, discrepancies occasionally occur among researchers' findings, some of which will be noted in the ensuing pages.

For the three decades immediately preceding 1978, the birth of the NKPA had been commemorated on 8 February—the date its modern military force was established in 1948.[4] Then in 1978 North Korea changed the commemoration date of the NKPA's commencement to 25 April to correspond with the date in 1932 that Kim Il Sung allegedly organized his Anti-Japanese Guerrilla Army.[5] By this act, North Korea was declaring that Kim Il Sung's anti-Japanese army was the primordial organization of the NKPA. Likewise, this act can be viewed as an attempt to extol the Korean-ness of the NKPA, while dismissing the combined influences of the Soviets and the Chinese Communists upon the establishment of the NKPA.

RESEARCH OBJECTIVES

As a means of understanding the thesis topic—the origins and current tactics of the NKPA—this book examines the following questions; namely:

1. What is the historical context in which the NKPA was established, including (a) Korea's anti-Japanese partisan history from 1931 to 1945, and (b) the Soviet liberation and occupation of North Korea from 1945 to 1948?
2. When and how was the NKPA organized, including (a) who were its leaders and what were their collective influences upon the organization; (b) how was the NKPA's manpower assessed; (c) how was the NKPA equipped, particularly regarding its acquisition of heavy weaponry; and (d) how was the army trained, including the basis of its doctrine, the formation of its domestic military training and education bases, and the receipt of foreign military training?
3. How did the Chinese Communists and Soviets contribute to the development of the NKPA prior to the beginning of the Korean War?
4. How has the NKPA evolved since 1950?
5. What are the current military strategies and tactics of the NKPA?

LIMITATIONS

Although personal language limitations restricted my research of this book to the use of primary sources in English or Korean, the use of secondary English-language sources aided in expanding the research to include Chinese, Japanese, and Russian insights into the topic.

SOURCES

Among the scores of published materials used in this study, a few sources were clearly indispensable, including several South Korean and North Korean publications, three books by North Korean defectors, and a few English-language publications, including U.S. government reports.

In 1985 the Republic of Korea Army (ROKA) began revising its perceived understanding of the military tactics of the NKPA. This revision was made possible by the assistance of a North Korean defector and about thirty procured North Korean reference materials. Then in 1997, with the use of many more important North Korean reference materials, ROKA refined its interpretation of NKPA tactics and in January 2000 published a new threat manual. This new reference manual, which is titled *Chŏk ŭl alcha* [Let us understand the enemy] offers an in-depth perspective on how the NKPA fights. This manual and the Republic of Korea Ministry of National Defense's *Kukpang Paeksŏ: 2004* [Defense White Paper: 2004] provided unique insight into the NKPA, particularly as it pertains to its current organization.

Whereas a voluminous collection of North Korean literature exists about its partisan period and its postliberation era, books that have been published since the late 1960s are heavily imbued with propaganda, thus voiding them of impartiality. Among the earlier extent publications used in this study was Im Ch'un-ch'u, *Hangil mujaeng t'ujaeng sigirŭl hoe-sang hayŏ* [Recollecting the times of the anti-Japanese armed struggle], published in 1960. Im, a subordinate of Kim Il Sung in the NEAJUA, chronicles many experiences from this period. In Im's recollections, he states that Kim Il Sung's superior officer, Wei Zhengmin, directed the founding of the Fatherland Restoration Association (FRA) and the Korean People's Revolutionary Army (KPRA), rather than Kim himself. As a result, Im's volume became one of many books that were later purged from North Korea. Another revealing work is Pak Tal's 1960 autobiography, *Choguk ŭn saengmyŏng poda tŏ kwijung hada* [The fatherland is more precious than life]. Pak Tal, an associate of Kim Il Sung, in

1935 co-organized (with Pak Kŭm-chŏl) the Kapsan Operation Committee, a Communist organization, which he later reorganized in 1937 as the Korean National Liberation Union, under the direction of Kim Il Sung.

An insightful collection of official speeches by Kim Il Sung was first published between 1953 and 1954 as a four-volume set and was titled *Kim Il Sung Sŏnjip* [Selected works of Kim Il Sung]. This work was later expanded as a six-volume edition and republished between 1960 and 1964. Another important work was written by Kim Il Sung's official biographer, Paek Pong (also Baik Bong). Titled *Minjok ŭi t'aeyang Kim Il Sung Changgun* [General Kim Il Sung the sun of the nation], it was first published in 1968 and then republished three years later. By juxtaposing these two volumes, the reader is able to detect factual alterations, which appear to be fabrications of the state's historiography.

North Korean defectors provide a rare and personal insight into North Korea's early political history. Some writers are discernibly emotional in their discourse, such as Lim Ŭn [Hŏ Chin] in his 1982 book *The Founding of a Dynasty in North Korea: An Authentic Biography of Kim Il-sŏng*. Lim Ŭn, a Soviet Korean who participated in North Korean politics, wrote from exile in the former Soviet Union about the "true nature" of Kim Il Sung. This book is an English translation of Lim's original work, which was published in Japanese and titled *A Secret History of the Founding of a North Korean Dynasty.*

Other important contributors to this field have remained relatively dispassionate in their writing style, lending a sense of impartiality to their work. Included among such writers is Kim Ch'ang-sun (also Kim Chang-soon), *Pukhan sibonyŏnsa* [Fifteen-year history of North Korea] (1961). Kim Ch'ang-sun was a former Communist reporter who used his personal insights to provide a political history of North Korea from 1945 to 1960. He later served as the director of the Institute for North Korean Studies, located in South Korea. Another relatively dispassionate author was Han Chae-dŏk, who published *Hanguk ŭi kongsan chuŭi wa pukhan ŭi yŏksa* [Korean Communism and the history of North Korea] in 1965. Han Chae-dŏk was a former North Korean journalist for the North Korean newspaper *Minju Chosŏn* and had personal contacts with Kim Il Sung after 1945. Han later defected to South Korea several years before his death in 1970.

In 1972 professors Robert A. Scalapino and Chong-sik Lee published a two-volume seminal work titled *Communism in Korea.* A portion of this book, which was particularly relevant to the current study, examines the NKPA through the recollections of Yi Ki-gŏn as recorded in an interview with Chong-sik Lee in 1969. Yi Ki-gŏn was a Korean native who trained at the Manchukuo Military Academy before national liberation. A lieutenant colonel in the 1st NKPA Division, he defected to South Korea in 1948.

The use of English-language sources broadened the scope of this study in that they often included works that relied extensively upon foreign-language sources and intelligence records. For instance, U.S. intelligence records were used expansively by Roy E. Appleman (1961) and Bruce Cumings (1981, 1990); Chinese sources were used by Chen Jian (1994), Nie Rongzhen (1989), and Suh Dae-Sook (1988); Japanese sources were employed by Sadako N. Ogata (1964) and Suh Dae-Sook (1988); and Soviet sources were used by Fania Isaakovna Shabshina (1951) and Erik Van Ree (1989).

Viewed in its entirety, and cited often in this work, is a declassified U.S. Department of State intelligence report titled *North Korea: A Case Study in the Techniques of Take-over.* Originally produced in May 1951, and then declassified and published in 1961, this document represents the findings of a State Department research mission that was sent to Korea in October 1950 to conduct a survey of the North Korean regime as it had operated before the outbreak of hostilities on 25 June 1950.

To provide further enlightenment on the sources used in this work, an annotated bibliography is included.

SIGNIFICANCE OF THE STUDY

In August 1945 the Soviet Red Army liberated the northern portion of Korea, ending Japan's thirty-five-year colonization of the Korean peninsula. Within three years, the northern part of Korea, with the assistance of its Soviet liberators, erected a new Communist state. On the southern portion of the peninsula, the United States assisted in the establishment of a democratic state. In June 1950 North Korea conducted an ill-fated attack across its southern border with the intent of reunifying the peninsula under its Communist banner.

On the surface, the Korean War may not seem much different from any other war. After all, war in its most simplistic form is little more than the act of leaders maneuvering men and equipment against an opponent in battle to achieve certain objectives. In this regard, the Korean War, which lasted from 1950 to 1953, has been well chronicled; however, the treatment of how the NKPA was organized before the outbreak of hostilities is still a rather recondite topic, as is the subject of how the NKPA currently fights. An understanding of these topics requires, first, an examination into the methods that were employed to man, equip, and train the NKPA, including domestic and international involvement; and, second, a review of the NKPA's strategy, doctrine, and tactics.

Although there are several important works that contain insights into the origins of the NKPA, very few, if any, English-language volumes exclusively address this topic, as is also the case with NKPA tactics. This book hopes to fill that void. For this purpose alone, the present work bears relevance, particularly among students of Korean history and those seeking a deeper understanding of the NKPA, but unequivocally it is required reading for every United States soldier, sailor, airman, marine, and military planner who must remain prepared to rapidly deploy to Korea then close with and destroy this most dangerous of enemies.

TRANSLITERATION

The McCune-Reischauer transliteration system is used for Korean, with a few exceptions, including Kim Il Sung's name, which uses the accepted English form. The Pinyin Romanization system is used for Chinese; however, popular names have traditional Wade-Giles spellings in parenthesis, following first use. A modified version of the Hepburn system is used for Japanese, and a modified version of the Library of Congress system is used for Russian transliterations.

Part 1

Origins

ORDER OF MILITARY SERVICE AND HONOR MEDAL
(Kunsa Pongmu Yŭngye Metal)

The ribbon on the Order of Military Service and Honor Medal has five stripes, alternating red, yellow, green, yellow, and red. The medal is a 33-mm-diameter silver disk with Mount P'aektu on the top with radiant beams emanating from behind it. In the foreground, from left to right, are the busts of a soldier, sailor, and pilot. On the obverse, written in Korean, are the words *Kunsa Pongmu Yŭngye Metal*. (Art by Matthew S. Minnich).

1

Early Origins of the (North) Korean People's Army: Partisan Lineage

SINCE AT LEAST February 1948, when Kim Il Sung delivered his inaugural speech to the (North) Korean People's Army (NKPA), North Korea has officially recognized his former Anti-Japanese Guerrilla Army as the predecessor to the nation's modern armed forces. To this end, the North Korean state has attempted to create a single, uninterrupted history that traces Kim Il Sung from independent leader of the Anti-Japanese Guerrilla Army in 1932—later renamed the Korean People's Revolutionary Army—to supreme commander of the NKPA in 1948. Regardless of its degree of authenticity, North Korea officially endorses this historiography as the NKPA's true lineage, and despite many factual discrepancies that are evident in this contrived history (as will be revealed throughout this book), there is indeed a thread of truth to this idea.

Certainly a great number of NKPA soldiers and leaders, including Kim Il Sung, did hail from a partisan background, including service with Chinese Communist guerrillas in Manchuria and the Soviet Red Army in the Soviet Far East. Thus, roots of North Korea's modern era, including origins of the NKPA, can be found in this partisan period between the early 1930s and the early 1940s. It was during this time that the country's future leaders were trained in the art of command, that its men became battle-hardened, and that these neighboring Communist states—China and North Korea—forged enduring associations and bonds.

What follows is a reconstruction of North Korea's partisan period from the Manchurian Incident or Mukden Incident of 1931 until Korea's national liberation in 1945.* This account clearly deconstructs the myth of the NKPA's heritage; namely, that its antecedent organization operated as an independent army under the leadership of Kim Il Sung from its inception in 1932 until national liberation in 1945. At the same time, it explains the effect that this period later had upon the NKPA, particularly as it pertained to the selection of its senior leaders, who for the most part were all *Kapsan* Partisans (Soviet exiles), or *Kapsanists*–including Kim Il Sung.[†]

ANTI-JAPANESE GUERRILLA ARMY

Immediately following the Manchurian Incident of 18 September 1931, Japan's *Kantōgun* (Guandong or Kwantung Army) moved quickly to annex Manchuria. Japan's provocations emboldened the Communists to fight back, prompting a rapid growth in guerrilla units. Apparently, one such example of organized resistance occurred in November 1931 when a group of Communists convened for ten days in Mingyuekou, Yanji County (Korean: Myŏngwŏlgu, Yŏn'gil Hyŏn), Manchuria, to discuss a plan for mobilizing local manpower for the purpose of creating guerrilla units. Kim Il Sung, who was reportedly present at that meeting, was tasked with enlisting volunteers in Antu County (k: Ando Hyŏn), Manchuria—where he and his ailing mother resided.[1] According to North Korean literature, Kim Il Sung successfully organized a group of young men into a partisan unit in 1932. Such literature refers to this group as an "anti-Japanese people's partisan unit," and although these works indicate that the unit was organized in eastern Manchuria, there is no mention of the exact date of its activation.[2] In 1963 North Korean literature specified that the unit was formed in April 1932,[3] and in 1968, Paek Pong, Kim Il Sung's official biographer, recounted events as

---

* On 18 September 1931, a bomb exploded at a Japanese railway near Mukden (modern day Shenyang), an incident exploited by the Japanese Kantōgun army as a pretext to occupy southern Manchuria and eventually erect the puppet state of Manchukuo in February 1932.
† Chong-sik Lee is the first to taxonomize Kim Il Sung's partisan group as the "Kapsan faction." Chong-sik Lee, "Korean Communists and Yenan," *The China Quarterly*, no. 9 (January–March 1962), 182–192.

follows: "Having completed basic [military] preparation, the General [Kim Il Sung] brought together revolutionary workers, peasants, and patriotic youth of Antu, Yanji and Helong, with eighteen excellent young fighters including Ch'a Kwang-su, who, from the beginning, had been raised in the Communist Youth League, forming the core, and proclaimed the formation of the Anti-Japanese Guerrilla Army [*Han'gil Yugyŏktae*] in Antu. The day was 25 April 1932." Thereafter, the general dispatched other comrades to organize guerrilla units in the eastern Manchurian counties of Wangqing, Hunchun, Yanji, and Helong. Concurrently, other Korean Communists in both north and south Manchuria were likewise establishing guerrilla units.[4]

During the 1930s, many small Korean and Chinese guerrilla units emerged throughout Manchuria. On a larger scale, in January 1932 the Manchurian Provincial Committee of the Chinese Communist Party (CCP) in Harbin directed Chinese partisan Yang Jingyu to establish the Thirty-second Red Army (later renamed the First Army) in Panshi County by recruiting local Chinese and Korean inhabitants. Over the next two years this committee directed the creation of five more armies, including the Second Army, which had a heavy concentration of Korean guerrilla fighters and was commanded by a Korean partisan named Chu Chin.[5]

Apparently, a few years after the formation of Kim's Anti-Japanese Guerrilla Army, Kim named the unit the Korean People's Revolutionary Army (KPRA), or *Chosŏn Inmin Hyŏgmyŏnggun*. However, there are many factual discrepancies about its origin. In their book *Communism in Korea*, professors Robert Scalapino and Chong-sik Lee state that the KPRA was created in May 1934.[6] Professor Dae-Sook Suh, on the other hand, states in his exceptionally well-written book *Kim Il Sung* that the KPRA was formed in March 1934.[7] Admittedly, the difference between these two accounts is hardly significant and probably represents no more than a typographical error. A significant gaffe is exposed, however, by reviewing North Korea's official historiography.

In the first edition of Kim Il Sung's official biography, Paek Pong writes that in February 1936, General Kim Il Sung—who was present at a meeting of military and political cadre in Nanhudou, Ningan County, Manchuria (k: Namhodu, Yŏngan Hyŏn)—proposed the foundation of a Marxist-Leninist Party, the formation of a stronger anti-Japanese national united front, and the relocation of guerrilla units into Korea's northern border area. Paek goes on to state that after the Nanhudou Conference, Kim Il Sung led his Anti-Japanese Guerrilla Army to the northern border area, where it was renamed the KPRA before continuing on to Tonggang, Fusong County, Manchuria (k: Tonggang, Musong Hyŏn), where he arrived in early May 1936.[8] Assuming this information to be accurate, the KPRA would have been established sometime between February and May 1936.

However, the year after Paek Pong introduced his biography of Kim Il Sung, the Party History Institute of the Central Committee of the Workers' Party of Korea published the *Brief History of the Revolutionary Activities of Comrade Kim Il Sung,* which submitted as fact an entirely different account of when the KPRA was founded. According to this account, "In March 1934 Comrade Kim Il Sung organized the Korean People's Revolutionary Army by reforming the organizational system of the Anti-Japanese Guerrilla Army in order to further strengthen and develop the anti-Japanese armed struggle."[9]

In the years between 1971 and 1976 Paek Pong published a new edition of his biography of Kim Il Sung. In the third volume of this new edition, Paek Pong included in the chronological table a brief entry stating that "in March 1934 the Anti-Japanese Guerrilla Army was organized into the Korean People's Revolutionary Army."[10] In the revised first volume he removed the statement that the KPRA was organized in 1936 and inserted, several chapters earlier in the book, that "in March 1934 [Kim Il Sung] reorganized the Anti-Japanese Guerrilla Army's system of organization forming the Korean People's Revolutionary Army."[11]

Accurate or otherwise, it appears that at least since 1969 North Korea has recognized March 1934 as the date that General Kim Il Sung renamed the Anti-Japanese Guerrilla Army the Korean People's Revolutionary Army.

This exposure that North Korean historiographers have contrived certain facts about the formation of the KPRA is not presented to refute the existence of such a military unit, for it is certain that Kim Il Sung did indeed command a partisan unit during the mid-1930s. What is more suspect is whether he actually organized this unit or the many other groups that he purportedly established. Perhaps, then, this example shows the difficulty with which the North Korean state has combined events and chronology to fabricate a credible Kim Il Sung myth—a chronicle wherein everything begins and ends with Kim Il Sung–in an attempt to establish a claim of political legitimacy.

In the summer of 1935 the Seventh Comintern Congress met in Moscow for the purpose of creating an anti-Japanese united front. The CCP responded by issuing the August First Declaration—a statement of endorsement that precipitated the merger of the six armies of the Manchurian Provincial Committee of the CCP into the Northeast Anti-Japanese United Army (NEAJUA), or *Dongbei Kangri Lianjun,* on 20 February 1936.[12]

That same month, Kim Il Sung led the KPRA from Nanhudou toward Tonggang, Fusong County, an arduous march of some 180 miles over difficult, snow-covered terrain.[13] Stopping in Mihunchen (k: Mihonjin), Antu County (approximately halfway to Tonggang), in March, the NEAJUA apparently designated Kim Il Sung's partisan forces, the so-called KPRA, as the 3rd Division (later 6th Division) of the Second Army of the NEAJUA and concurrently appointed Kim as its division commander.[14] Although North Korean historiographers have deliberately omitted any mention that Kim Il Sung's KPRA was in fact a subordinate unit of the NEAJUA, earlier North Korean literature— including Im Ch'un-ch'u's chronicles and Pak Tal's autobiography*— corroborates the fact that Kim Il Sung was the 3rd Division (later 6th Division) commander of the NEAJUA.[15]

Proceeding southwest through Mengjiang (currently Jingyou) (k: Man'gang), Fusong County, and then northwest to Tonggang, Kim Il Sung arrived there in early May, where he allegedly participated in a fifteen-day conference. Reportedly, "on 5 May 1936, during the height of the Tonggang Conference, the Fatherland Restoration Association [FRA], or *Choguk Kwangbokhoe,* was formed, being Korea's first single-mass, anti-Japanese united front organization."[16] Furthermore, it was purported that "at that meeting, Kim Il Sung was elected chairman of the association."[17]

Some North Korean writings have recorded that during the Tong-gang Conference, Kim Il Sung presented the FRA's inaugural declaration, a ten-point program, and a set of rules, all of which he allegedly

---

* An associate of Kim Il Sung, in 1935 Pak Tal organized the Kapsan Operational Committee, a Communist organization, which he reorganized in 1937 as the Korean National Liberation Union as directed by Kim Il Sung.

authored during his "long march" to Tonggang. Lacking explicit Communist overtones, these documents were apparently intended to accentuate nationalistic feelings among the various anti-Japanese Korean partisan units (see appendix B). The formation of the FRA was in response to the CCP's August First Declaration, which directed the building of an anti-Japanese united front. North Korea claims that within a few months of the inauguration of this organization, more than two hundred thousand members joined the FRA, with branches quickly emerging in scores of villages throughout Manchuria and Korea.[18]

As membership increased in the NEAJUA, these armies spawned a total of eleven armies that in order to enhance command and control were operationally grouped into the First, Second, and Third Route Armies.[19] Assembled in the First Route Army were the First and Second Armies; in the Second Route Army were the Fourth, Fifth, Seventh, Eighth, and Tenth Armies; and in the Third Route Army were the Third, Sixth, Ninth, and Eleventh Armies. Inasmuch as the majority of the guerrilla fighters were Chinese, the majority of NEAJUA's leaders were likewise Chinese, although certainly not exclusively so. Included among the NEAJUA leadership were the following Koreans: division commanders An Pong-hak, Ch'oe Hyŏn, and Kim Il Sung (promoted to army commander in 1938); army political commissars Chŏn Kwang, Ch'oe Yong-gŏn, Kim Ch'aek, and Yi Hong-gwang;* and army commanders Chu Chin and Yi Hak-man.[20]

While unit sizes greatly varied, NEAJUA divisional forces were typically composed of one hundred to three hundred personnel. Kim Il Sung initially commanded the 3rd Division of the Second Army of the NEAJUA; however, when the First and Second Armies were combined under the First Route Army,[21] the designation of Kim's division was changed to the 6th Division.[22] The 6th Division had approximately two hundred riflemen, fifty grenadiers, and two light machine gunners.[23]

Guerrilla combat techniques were the forte of the NEAJUA; hence, battles fought were predominantly small in scale and short in duration. North Korea's most highly acclaimed partisan battle occurred on 4 June 1937 in the North Korean border town of Poch'ŏnbo. This battle was significant because of its psychological effect rather than any quantitative,

* Yi Hong-gwang served as 1st NEAJUA Division commander from November 1934 until his death in March 1935.

physical effect. Indeed, Kim's division killed fewer than seven Japanese police officers, including Police Chief Ōkawa Shuichi.[24] Nevertheless, the Poch'ŏnbo raid and the events that occurred in proximity to it boosted Kim Il Sung's fame as a great guerrilla fighter. The Koreans extolled the success of this raid through newspaper reports and by word of mouth. The Japanese responded by increasing the bounty on Kim's head to the equivalent of one hundred thousand dollars.[25]

From the Japanese invasion of Manchuria in September 1931 until the defeat of the NEAJUA in March 1941, tens of thousands of Chinese and Korean partisans devoted their lives to restoring independence to their homeland.[26] By the spring of 1941 the *Kantōgun* had defeated the NEAJUA, forcing many of the guerrilla fighters to flee to the Soviet maritime provinces of Primorsky and Khabarovsky Krai, where many of them were assimilated into the Soviet military.[27]

Although collectively these partisan armies failed to defeat the Japanese invaders, individually many survived, and having endured the hardships of war and subjugation, the end of World War II witnessed the eventual elevation of many survivors to esteemed positions of public service in their respective national governments.

KOREAN INDEPENDENT LEAGUE AND THE KOREAN VOLUNTEER ARMY

The origin of the NKPA is certainly rooted in the anti-Japanese guerrilla armies in general, and specifically in the forces of Kim Il Sung, as well as those of Mu Chŏng and Kim Tu-bong of the *Yanan* (Yenan) Group. Having already addressed the origins of Kim Il Sung's *Kapsanists*, it is equally important to examine the roots of the *Yanan* Group.

The North China Korean Independence League (NCKIL), or *Hwapuk Chosŏn Tongnip Tongmaeng,* had its roots in an earlier organization named the Korean National Revolutionary Party (KNRP), which was an amalgamated group of Korean Communists and nationalists that formed in Nanjing, China, in July 1935. A moderate leftist named Kim Wŏn-bong headed the KNRP, and the military arm of the party was called the Korean Volunteer Army (KVA), or *Chosŏn Ŭiyonggun.* The KNRP had been established to unify overseas Koreans in their anti-Japanese struggles, but policy differences contributed to the party's dissolution in

1937. In its stead, two new parties were formed: Ch'oe Ch'ang-ik organized the leftists into the Korean National Front; and Kim Ku formed the rightist Korean Independence Party (KIP).

After the Sino-Japanese War started in July 1937, the Korean National Front relocated to Yanan—the Chinese Communist capital—and the KIP followed the Chinese nationalists to Chongqing. In January 1941 the Korean National Front dissolved, and in its place the North China Korean Youth Federation (NCKYF) was formed in collaboration with the Korean Communists in that area. In August 1942 many members of Kim Ku's KIP migrated north to participate in the NCKYF's armed struggle against the Japanese forces. This led to the creation of yet another organization, the North China Korean Independence League (NCKIL).[28]

As a member of Mao Zedong's Chinese Communist Forces (CCF), Kim Tu-bong headed the NCKIL with Ch'oe Ch'ang-ik and Han Pin as vice chairmen.[29] The NCKIL's military arm, the KVA, was initially a small unit of about three to four hundred members commanded by Mu Chŏng.[30] Before joining the Chinese Communist Eighth Route Army and assuming command of the KVA, Mu Chŏng had graduated from Henan Military Academy of the Chinese Nationalist Army.[31]

Like Kim Tu-bong and Mu Chŏng, Koreans who served among the CCF were labeled *Yananists,* a term that identified them as hailing from Yanan, China—their base of origin. Included in the *Yananists* was a military unit that called itself the Yi Hong-gwang Detachment (YHD), or *Yi Hong-gwang Chidae.* It should be remembered that Yi Hong-gwang was a Manchurian-based Korean guerrilla who fought with the NEAJUA during the 1930s. The YHD and the KVA were the only two distinctively Korean partisan units that continued to function until their return to Korea after its liberation in 1945.[32]

SOVIET TRAINING PERIOD, 1941-1945

Fleeing from the Japanese *Kantōgun,* several surviving members of the NEAJUA arrived in the Soviet maritime provinces in early 1941. Upon their arrival, most were detected by the Soviet border guards and incarcerated until their identities could be established. Among the incarcerated was Kim Il Sung, who was reportedly held until he was identified by Zhou Baozhong, former Second Route Army commander of the NEAJUA.[33]

That same year, the Soviets activated the 88th Special Brigade, which was a special reconnaissance unit under the command of the Far East District Army. This unit was established for the purpose of conducting small-unit intelligence collection missions across the Soviet border. The brigade leadership was heavily organized around the former leadership of the NEAJUA. Zhou Baozhong was appointed as brigade commander, Major Serjokin as vice commander, and Major Shilinsky as chief of staff, the latter two men being Soviet officers. Many members of the brigade's senior leadership went on to become prominent *Kapsanists,* including: Ch'oe Yong-gŏn as the brigade political commissar; Kim Il Sung and Kang Kŏn as commanders of the 1st and 4th Battalions, respectively; An Kil as the 2nd Battalion political commissar; Kim Ch'aek as the 3rd Battalion vice commander; and Ch'oe Hyŏn, Ch'oe Yong-jin, Kim Il, and Kim Kwang-hyŏp as company commanders.[34] Leading Soviet Korean figures in the brigade included Hŏ Ka-i, Nam Il, and Pak Ch'ang-ik.[35] Of the 88th Special Brigade's 300 men, about 250 were Soviet Koreans; the remainder were *Kapsanists.*[36]

Han Chae-dŏk, a former journalist for the North Korean newspaper *Minju Chosŏn* (Korean Democracy), confirms that Kim Il Sung and his small band of partisans fled to the Soviet Union. In his book *Korean Communism and the History of North Korea* (1965), Han recorded the results of his August 1947 interview with Kim Il Sung, stating: "In 1941 Kim Il Sung and his military unit escaped to the Soviet Far East from Manchuria while being pursued by Japan's *Kantōgun.* While hiding in the Soviet Union for four years, he served in the Soviet Army. He returned to Korea in 1945 wearing the uniform of a Soviet major [*sojwa* 少佐]."[37] Han Chae-dŏk went on to say that Kim Il Sung felt embarrassed about having fled to the Soviet Union and that he avoided all further discussions on the matter.

Whether from embarrassment or because of a state-sponsored attempt to apotheosize Kim Il Sung, since the mid-1960s the North Korean government has purposefully omitted all references to the fact that Kim Il Sung and his *Kapsanists* took refuge in the Soviet Union, where they joined the 88th Special Brigade. Instead, this four-year period is depicted as a time of small-unit activities, or *sobudae hwaltong,* conducted from secret camps located near the Soviet border.[38]

MILITARY MERIT MEDAL
(Kun'gong Metal)
Established 13 June 1949

Awarded for meritorious action, the ribbon of the Military Merit Medal has nine stripes, alternating blue, white, red, white, blue, white, red, white, and blue. The medal is a 33-mm-diameter silver disk with the DPRK flag in the background and an infantryman in the foreground. On the obverse, written in Korean, are the words Kun'gong Metal. (Art by Matthew S. Minnich)

• 2 •

Birth of a Nation and Its Army:
The Soviets at the Helm

ALTHOUGH THE NKPA fondly traces its lineage through its anti-Japanese partisan period, the collective contributions of this era upon the growth of the NKPA greatly pale in comparison to the wide-sweeping effects that the Soviets had upon the army's expansion, particularly from 1945 to 1948. During this period, as national liberators the Soviet Red Army exercised expansive control over most aspects of the North Korean administration, including its national security. Professor Charles Armstrong of Columbia University correctly articulated the degree of Soviet control over North Korea during this period when he wrote, "The Soviets had control *in what mattered to them,* in particular North Korea's foreign policy, trade, and the maintenance of a generally pro-Soviet leadership [emphasis added)].... The Soviets also strongly influenced personnel and security structures."[1] One of the more enduring actions the Soviets took in shaping the NKPA was their decision to embrace and endorse Kim Il Sung as North Korea's preeminent political leader. With this endorsement, Kim Il Sung quickly empowered his small cohort of trusted colleagues—the *Kapsan* Partisans or *Kapsanists*—as the core leadership of the developing NKPA. Kim Il Sung's most trusted lieutenants, including Ch'oe Yong-gŏn, Kim Ch'aek, An Kil, Ch'oe Hyŏn, and Kang Kŏn, worked closely with the Soviet army leadership in incrementally adapting the Soviet military model, where applicable, in the development of the NKPA. This process included creating organizations, establishing education and training facilities, teaching doctrine, and outfitting units with individual and organizational equipment to include rifles, tanks, planes, and ships.

Despite the fact that the Soviet army served as an appropriate standard for modeling the formation of the NKPA, it was neither practical nor advisable to mime it in its entirety. Whereas the Soviet army organization model was centered on both armored and mechanized forces, neither Korea's mountainous terrain nor the perceived threat of its principal adversary—South Korea—warranted the great expenditure that such an armor-heavy force would have cost. Rather, NKPA divisions were organized with a focus on their infantry units, which had been schooled in Soviet doctrine at the newly established Korean-based training facilities. When considered holistically, the process of inaugurating the NKPA on 8 February 1948 appears mundane; however, when the Soviets entered North Korea in early August 1945, thirty-eight years to the month had elapsed since Korea last fielded its own army.[2] Hence, the Soviets' decision to build the NKPA was accompanied by the realization that the task would have to begin from scratch, since North Korea had no military formations, combat equipment, or leadership trained in the art of modern warfare. Consequently, the crux of understanding the origins of the NKPA is predicated on an awareness of North Korea's Soviet-centric, post-liberation era, which began in August 1945 and lasted just three short years; this chapter is a condensed examination of that historical period.

LIBERATION

By late July 1945, 590,000 troops of the Soviet Union's Far Eastern High Command (3,000 of which were ethnic Koreans),[3] including a three-army front and a maritime fleet, confronted the Japanese *Kantōgun* in Manchuria and the Japanese Seventeenth Front in Korea, which equated to a combined force of a comparable strength.[4] A few days later, on 6 August 1945, the United States dropped its first atomic bomb on

Hiroshima, Japan. Emboldened by the success of this attack, Soviet premier Joseph Stalin authorized the Far Eastern High Command to attack the defending Japanese forces on 9 August—less than twenty-four hours after declaring war against Japan.[5] In the heavy rains of 9 August, the Red Army crossed the Soviet-Manchurian border at 1:00 AM. Quickly moving against the Japanese forces, advanced divisions of the Soviet Twenty-fifth Army, commanded by Col. Gen. Ivan Mikhailovich Chistiakov, crossed the Soviet-Korean border on the night of 11–12 August, while amphibious forces secured ports at Unggi and Najin.[6] Then, following a two-day naval bombardment of the port city Ch'ŏngjin, Soviet troops landed on its beach and fought their toughest fight for the liberation of Korea from 13 to 16 August. Although the Japanese surrender was announced on 15 August, fighting in Manchuria and Korea did not cease until five days later.[7] On 25 August 1945 Marshal Kirill Afanasievich Meretskov, commander of the First Far Eastern Front,* informed Chistiakov that the Twenty-fifth Army would serve as the occupation force of North Korea.[8]

As Soviet forces spread through Korea, they established local commander bureaus called *komendaturas* for the principal purpose of maintaining local order.[9] *Komendaturas* then encouraged the establishment of local self-rule councils, or people's committees (*inmin wiwŏnhoe-dŭl*), and associated security units (*ch'iandae-dŭl*).[10]

By the end of the war, Soviet forces had only slightly penetrated northern Korea, while the area below the 38th parallel was reserved for occupation by the American forces, as had been earlier agreed upon by Stalin and American president Harry S. Truman. Therefore, as an interim measure, until the new Soviet and American military governments could arrive, the Japanese authorities transferred political power to certain prominent Koreans and asked them to organize a provisional government. Accordingly, on 15 August 1945 the so-called Committee for the Preparation of Korean Independence (CPKI), or *Chosŏn Kŏn'guk Chunbi Wiwŏnhoe,* was established in Seoul, with separate branches throughout all thirteen provinces on the peninsula,[11] including the P'yŏngyang branch, which was organized by Cho Man-sik, a respected conservative nationalist. Immediately following the Soviet

---

* Formerly the Maritime Army Group, on 2 August 1945 it was renamed the First Far Eastern Front.

occupation of P'yŏngyang, the P'yŏngyang branch of the CPKI was dissolved because of its 90 percent non-Communist membership. It was subsequently reorganized with an equal number of Communist members as the People's Political Committee, or *Inmin Chŏngch'i Wiwŏnhoe.*[12] This pattern of assuring Communist membership parity in people's committees then further spread throughout North Korea.

Because of the rapidity with which the war ended in August 1945, many Soviet ground forces never maneuvered against the defending Japanese units, as was apparently the case with the 88th Special Brigade. This reconnaissance unit, which stood postured to deploy from Soviet military bases in Khabarovsk, Okeanskaia, and Vladivostok, included among its ranks such famous *Kapsanists* as Kim Il Sung, Ch'oe Yong-gŏn, and Kim Ch'aek.[13] Although North Korean historiography depicts Kim Il Sung leading the Korean People's Revolutionary Army in a battle to liberate Korea alongside the Soviet army, Lim Ŭn, a Soviet Korean who participated in North Korean politics, insists that Kim Il Sung, along with fifty other partisans, was merely transported to Korea by ship after the cessation of hostilities.[14] Lim Ŭn also states that upon being repatriated on 19 September 1945 these men were directed to register with the *komendatura* in their former hometowns. Apparently, at this point Kim Il Sung, a Soviet army officer,[15] was appointed as deputy commander of the P'yŏngyang *Komendatura*—a political assignment.[16]

After the liberation of Korea in August 1945, returning Koreans from the Soviet Union were either *Kapsanists* or Soviet Koreans. *Kapsanists,* the smaller of these two groups—about two hundred people—were Korean partisans who fled with their families from Manchuria to the Soviet Union in the early 1940s.[17] The larger group—Soviet Koreans—describes some eight hundred thousand Korean émigrés who were former long-term Soviet residents,[18] including some three hundred thousand second- and third-generation Koreans from Uzbekistan and Kazakhstan.[19] In establishing civil administration in Korea, the Soviets employed many Soviet Koreans by relocating as many as thirty thousand people from nearby Siberia.[20] These loyal Soviet Koreans were familiar with Soviet ideology, which enabled the Soviets to quickly install a bilingual bureaucracy throughout the northern zone of occupation.[21]

During the first few weeks of occupation, the Soviets concentrated on stabilizing public orderliness and normality, which was greatly augmented by the emergence of the aforementioned self-rule people's committees and local security units. However, once the forty-thousand-strong occupation force of the Twenty-fifth Army was firmly ensconced on the peninsula, it began using its position of power to begin transforming North Korea into a Communist state.[22] Although this process was slow, it appears to have been deliberate. The next phase of this transitional work required transforming the Red Army from its role as liberator to that of civil administrator. Hence, in early October, just seven weeks after the first Soviet troops entered Korea, the Soviet Civil Administration, under the directorship of Maj. Gen. Andrei Alekseevich Romanenko, was established in North Korea by the Maritime Military District.[23] Dr. Erik Van Ree argues that the Soviet Civil Administration was subordinate to the Soviet Twenty-fifth Army, which, in every aspect functioned as the military government in North Korea.[24]

ROAD TO SELF-AUTONOMY

Consistent with Soviet intentions to quickly establish a friendly, indigenous Korean government, the Soviet Civil Administration promptly authorized the creation of a shadow Korean administration. To this end, Colonel General Chistiakov approved the assemblage of some 170 people, including participants from the Soviet command, the provincial people's committees, and other invited guests, including Kim Il Sung.[25] On 8 October 1945 this assembled body elected thirty representatives (fifteen Communists and fifteen nationalists) from five North Korean provinces for the purpose of organizing a quasi-political center (or shadow government).[26] Cho Man-sik, the nationalist group leader, was elected as chairman of the so-called Five North Korean Provinces' Administrative Bureau (FNKPAB), or *Pukchosŏn Odo Haengjŏngguk*. Completely organized by 10 November 1945, the FNKPAB was composed of ten subordinate bureaus, including the bureaus of industry, transportation, communication, agriculture and forestry, commerce, finance, education, public health, justice, and security (or *Poankuk*).[27] Even though FNKPAB was short-lived and curtailed in its authority, there were some obvious benefits from its existence, including valuable learning experience for several future government leaders. One of these was Ch'oe Yong-gŏn, the chief of the Security Bureau, who later rose to occupy the second highest position in North Korea's government—titular head of state.

With the establishment of the Soviet Civil Administration, ad hoc local security units were quickly devalued in importance to the Soviet command. As a result, on 12 October 1945, the day after the FNKPAB conference concluded, Colonel General Chistiakov issued an order dissolving all indigenous security organizations, including the public safety corps (*ch'iandae*), self-defense guards (*chawidae*), and the bodyguards (*ch'inwidae*). As recorded by Kim Ch'ang-sun, a former Communist who lived in North Korea during the early postwar period, that order included the following directives: "All armed militia units within North Korea will disband. All weapons, ammunition, and military supplies will be surrendered to a duty commander of the Soviet military or police. For maintenance of public order amongst the commoners, the provisional provincial committees [*imshi to wiwŏnhoe-dŭl*] will negotiate with the Soviet Army Headquarters for the approval to organize a *poandae,* of which the number of personnel will be prescribed."[28]

Essentially, this order was a purge of the volunteer police and had the affect of eliminating the non-Communists from this position of power. In its place the Soviets directed the creation of a pro-Communist centralized security organization, which was established by transferring two thousand Soviet Koreans from the occupation force to the "newly sanctioned" peace preservation corps (*poandae*) within each province.[29]

With a semblance of social order beginning to take hold, on 14 October 1945 the Soviets hosted a rally in P'yŏngyang to honor the Red Army as national liberators of Korea.[30] As a part of this gathering, Colonel General Chistiakov presented Kim Il Sung to the people as a national hero.[31] Delivering his first public speech since his repatriation, Kim Il Sung thanked the Soviets for liberating Korea and called upon all Koreans to unite in the task of building a new democratic Korea.[32] Van Ree suggests that during the assembly Kim might have spoken in his capacity as deputy commander of the P'yŏngyang *Komendatura*.[33] Another possibility is that Kim was recognized because of his position as first secretary of the recently established Northern Korean Bureau of the Korean Communist Party, which was established only the day before, on 13 October.[34] Regardless of the details surrounding Kim's invitation to speak that day, it appears that this rally was a defining moment in Kim's political rise.

With the disarm and disband order not more than two weeks old, the Soviets were presented with a new challenge as the main body of the KVA arrived at the Manchurian-Korean border. Returning from China, where the KVA had fought with the Chinese Eighth Route Army under the leadership of Mu Chŏng and Kim Tu-bong, Commander Kim Kang and Deputy Commander Kim Ho led their two-thousand-man unit of mostly new recruits to Korea.[35] As the group approached the Korean border, it was halted on the northwest side of the Amnok (Yalu) River in Dandong (Andong), Manchuria, by Soviet security forces. During the two weeks that followed, Soviet security forces detained the KVA as the Soviet Twenty-fifth Army deliberated on what to do. Finally the Twenty-fifth Army chief of staff, Lieutenant General V. A. Pen'kovsky, personally arrived on the southeast side of the Amnok River in Sinŭiju to resolve the situation.[36] At this point, according to Kim Ch'ang-sun, Pen'kovsky met with the unit's officers and authorized the KVA to enter Korea. However, after crossing the border and briefly parading through the town of Sinŭiju, the Soviet security force disarmed the KVA and returned the majority of its soldiers to Manchuria.[37]

There are perhaps several reasons why the Soviets treated the returning KVA forces this way. First among the possibilities is the concern that a trained, armed force of this magnitude might have been difficult to suppress once it was allowed unfettered access to the country. Also, in accordance with Soviet orders, all armed militias were to be "disarmed and disbanded." Second, as Kim Ch'ang-sun writes, many of these soldiers—although ethnically Korean—actually lived in Manchuria; hence, it is possible that the Soviets were regulating immigration with the goal of population control. A third possibility, as Scalapino and Lee have suggested, is that perhaps the Soviets' actions were politically motivated.[38] Since the *Yanan* Group shared close ties with China, it might have been considered prudent to suppress a political competitor with predispositions to see North Korea aligned more closely with China than with the

Soviet Union. Finally, most of these two thousand soldiers were actually raw recruits, and rather than repatriating them, perhaps they were encouraged to return to the Chinese Eighth Route Army so that after a period of seasoning they might return to Korea, to become a core element in the nation's future armed forces.[39]

MILITARY ACADEMIES AND TRAINING CENTERS

With the dissolution of all armed forces well under way, the Soviets turned their attention to the necessity of creating a new national security force. Kim Il Sung's biographer Paek Pong states that "in order to train new military and political cadre among workers and farmers, the north's first military-political school was founded in P'yŏngyang in November 1945."[40] The school was initially named the P'yŏngyang Institute, or P'yŏngyang *Hakwŏn,*[41] and *Kapsanist* Kim Ch'aek served as its first commandant, while the school's dean was Ki Sŏk-bok, a Soviet Korean who was educated at Leningrad State University.[42] The institute's principal instructors were Soviet Koreans who taught a two- to four-month course in political science, Communist history, and Russian language.[43]

Matriculating students were selected with the expectation that upon graduation they would fill one of the many leadership positions in North Korea's burgeoning state, including cadre positions in the Communist party, the *poandae,* and eventually within the military.[44] The first class graduated in the spring of 1946, whereupon graduating cadre members were assigned to serve in the newly created Railroad Guard forces, or *ch'ŏldo poandae.*[45] These forces had been established at the first of the year,[46] and within six months there were thirteen such companies organized and posted throughout every province to protect the country's railway services.[47] The expansion of the *poandae* necessitated the infusion of more trained cadres; hence, graduates from the second class were used to fill new cadre positions throughout the various provincial *poandae.* Inasmuch as many of the serving policemen were untrained, provinces were encouraged to send to training those who they determined were "sound in politics, thoughts, and morals."[48] By mid-1946 there were approximately 15,600 policemen serving in the *poandae,*[49] the majority of whom were affiliated with Communist youth groups.[50]

In the days and months after the FNKPAB Conference, several crucial events occurred. In Moscow the foreign minister equivalents of the United States, Great Britain, and the Soviet Union agreed to impose on Korea a trusteeship of up to five years, an idea that was vehemently rejected by many Koreans on both sides of the 38th parallel.[51] In P'yŏngyang, Major General Romanenko pressured Cho Man-sik to support a policy of Korean trusteeship as outlined in the Moscow Agreement. In the end, however, Cho would not acquiesce, which resulted in his arrest and the ultimate dissolution of the FNKPAB by early January 1946.

By February the Soviets had steered the Koreans into creating a Communist-centric, interim North Korean government.[52] On 8 February 1946 a grand conference assembled in P'yŏngyang to discuss the creation of a temporary central government. In attendance were leaders from the people's committees of North Korea's six provinces as well as the heads of the democratic parties and various social organizations.[53] Kim Il Sung opened the conference by advocating the virtues of establishing an interim government. Inaugurated later that day, the North Korean Interim People's Committee (NKIPC) was formed under the appointed leadership of Chairman Kim Il Sung and Vice Chairman Kim Tu-bong, the former leader of the KVA's Communist party—the Korean Independence League.[54] Additionally, Ch'oe Yong-gŭn remained in office as the chief of the Security Bureau, in charge of all police and security matters. With the establishment of an interim North Korean central government, the Soviet Civil Administration then naturally changed its role from administrator to advisor.

In the first months as its own master, North Korea sought the opportunity to expand its political position within the region by looking west to its Communist friends in China. Whereas the end of World War II at first brought peace to the Korean peninsula, it ultimately served to usher in a recommencement of hostilities between the Chinese nationalists and Communists as they initially battled for possession of Manchuria, an area that had only recently been vacated by the vanquished Japanese. During the next four years of China's civil war, North Korea proved to be an invaluable ally to the Chinese Communists.

In July 1946 P'yŏngyang sponsored a liaison office for the CCP's Northeast Bureau to fulfill four main missions: evacuating the wounded;

transferring materials; serving as a transportation and communication link between the CCF and Soviet forces in Dalian, China; and coordinating general North Korean assistance, including the purchase of war materials.[55] In short, North Korea served as a safe haven where the CCF could operate its strategic lines of communication outside the influence of the Chinese nationalist forces, a role that the Chinese Communists would later perform for North Korea, during the Korean War.

Concurrent with its assistance to the CCF, leading Korean Communists, who had adroitly seized central political power (with Soviet aid), moved quickly to create a military that could be relied upon to protect its political power monopoly. The decision to build a professional military, among other things, necessitated the creation of military training schools.

By July 1946 North Korea had opened its first exclusive military cadre (officer) training school, named the Central Security Cadre School, or *Chungang Poan Kanbu Hakkyo*.[56] The school's commandant was Ch'oe Yong-gŏn, who had earlier served as Security Bureau chief for the FNKPAB and later for the NKIPC.[57] Unlike the P'yŏngyang Institute, the Central Security Cadre School was exclusively a commissioning training course for uniformed military officers. Consequently, the school's program of instruction, which included courses on Soviet military tactics and Russian language, was more specialized than what was taught at the P'yŏngyang Institute.

On 15 August 1946, as Korea commemorated the first anniversary of its liberation from Japan, North Korea organized its first de facto military headquarters in P'yŏngyang, calling it the Security Cadre General Training Center (SCGTC), or *Poan Kanbu Ch'ong Hullyŏnso* (other sources refer to this organization as the Security Cadre's Training Battalion Headquarters, or *Poan Kanbu Hullyŏn Taedae Ponbu*).[58] As a military headquarters, the SCGTC was designated as the higher headquarters for the P'yŏngyang Institute, the Central Security Cadre School, and four newly formed military training centers, or *hullyŏnso-dŭl*.[59] Initially, the SCGTC also had an operational force that included three subordinate infantry battalions of four companies each that were posted in twelve towns throughout the country.[60]

Serving as commander of the SCGTC was *Kapsanist* Ch'oe Yong-gŏn, who concurrently served as commandant of the Central Security Cadre School and chairman of the Korean Democratic Party.[61] Other senior leaders of the organization included Kim Ch'aek as cultural commander (political commissar), An Kil as chief of staff, and Mu Chŏng as artillery commander.[62] With the exception of Mu Chŏng, who was a *Yananist,* these senior leaders were all *Kapsanists,* or Kim Il Sung loyalists. Undoubtedly, each officer was carefully selected to fill a specific billet. *Kapsanists* Ch'oe, Kim, and An were elevated to the most senior positions of trust and power, while Mu Chŏng, a non-*Kapsanist* and potential political rival to Kim Il Sung, was quietly marginalized by vesting him with a position of significantly less influence. This technique was often used in elevating *Kapsanists* over *Yananists,* Soviet Koreans, and natives.

By August 1946 North Korea had begun opening military training centers to teach basic military skills to new recruits.[63] These training centers were initially erected at former Japanese military bases in the towns of Kaech'ŏn, South P'yŏngan Province; Sinŭiju, North P'yŏngan Province; Nanam, North Hamgyŏng Province; and Wŏnsan, South Hamgyŏng Province.[64] Much of the military force received instruction at Korean training sites—commissioning schools and training centers—but other parts of the force were trained elsewhere. For example, in 1946 at least ten thousand North Korean youth were sent to Siberia for specialized military-technical training in avionics, tank gunnery, communications, and motor mechanics.[65]

Training centers were not used exclusively as training locations for military recruits; they also doubled as division-level operational headquarters. The First Security Cadre Training Center (later renamed the 1st NKPA Division) was located in Kaech'ŏn and was initially commanded by Kim Ŭng, a graduate of the Huangpu (Whampoa) Military Academy in Guangzhou (Canton), China. Kim Il served as the unit's cultural commander; Ch'oe Kwang was chief of staff; and Pak Kŭmchŏl, the original co-organizer (with Pak Tal) of the Kapsan Operation Committee, was a unit officer. Subordinate battalions (later elevated to regiments) were headquartered in the towns of Chŏngju (Yi Kwon-mu as commander), Kanggye (Ch'oe Hyŏn as commander), and Sinŭiju.

The Second Security Cadre Training Center (later renamed the 2nd NKPA Division) was located in Nanam and was initially commanded by Kang Kŏn.[66] With the exceptions of Kim Ŭng, who was a *Yananist,* and the Soviet Korean Yi Kwon-mu, these leaders were *Kapsanists.* This pattern of assigning former partisans to principal leadership positions throughout military and *poandae* units was a consistent policy.

Entrusting men to lead a nation's armed forces is serious business, and nowhere is it more critical than among emerging and developing states. Without a capable police force, internal anarchy can proliferate; likewise, without an adequate military force, neighboring countries may be enticed to invade. However, if unchecked in the hands of those that are ambitious or disgruntled, this same force can overthrow the government that empowers it. Both Kim Il Sung and his Soviet backers were well aware of this possibility and were therefore cautious in selecting *poandae* and military leaders. Hence, this small group of Kim Il Sung loyalists, or *Kapsanists* emerged as the core leadership of North Korea's armed forces.

The year 1946 witnessed more than just the embryonic growth of North Korea's ground forces; it also heralded the concurrent births of its aviation and maritime forces on 5 June 1946.[67] On this date, the Sinŭiju Aviation Unit, a civilian air service company, was designated a military aviation company and assigned to the P'yŏngyang Institute. Likewise, the fledgling naval organization, which was originally called the Maritime Security Corps Headquarters, was activated in Wŏnsan, South Hamgyŏng Province. That same month the Coast Guard Cadre School was founded in Wŏnsan to train a professional maritime border patrol. Within two months the Maritime Security Corps Headquarters was relocated to P'yŏngyang, where it was better able to control the security of both seacoasts. In the last month of 1946 the Maritime Security Corps was renamed the Coast Guard Corps. Later a second naval base was established in Chinnamp'o, which was eventually designated the headquarters for the Coast Guard Corps.[68]

By late 1946 Kim Il Sung had completed all preliminary steps in securing his base of power by controlling the government, the party, and the military, which by then had grown to a force of about twenty thousand, including the divisions at Kaech'ŏn (1st Division) and Nanam

(2nd Division),* the Chinnamp'o Brigade,[69] the Kanggye Artillery Regiment, and the Border Constabulary (*kyŏngbitae*) and Railroad Guards (*ch'ŏl poandae*).[70] Now all that remained was for Kim Il Sung to strengthen his grip on the burgeoning national power.

THE NATION AND ITS MILITARY

While concurrently building a reliable military, the North Korean Interim People's Committee set out to create a monolithic national Communist party, which culminated in the establishment of the North Korean Workers' Party (NKWP), or the *Pukchosŏn Nodongdang,* on 29 August 1946.[71] The NKWP was a merger of the Northern Korean Bureau of the Korean Communist Party,[72] under the leadership of Kim Il Sung, and Kim Tu-bong's recently established New People's Party, or *Sinmindang.* Established four months earlier, the New People's Party was a reorganization of Kim Tu-bong's Yanan-based Korean Independence League.[73]

As prescribed by the NKIPC, the first elections were held throughout North Korea on 3 November 1946 to elect representatives to each provincial, city, and county people's committee. On 17 February 1947 one-third of these representatives assembled in P'yŏngyang, with delegates from North Korea's Labor Party, Democratic Party, Religious Party (*Chŏngudang*), Trade Union, and Democratic Youth and Women's Leagues, in order to elect a legislative body called the People's Assembly of North Korea.[74] During the first session of the assembly, on 21 February, Kim Tu-bong was elected as standing chairman, with Ch'oe Yong-gŏn and Kim Tal-hyŏn as standing vice chairmen. During that same session, the People's Assembly renamed the NKIPC the North Korean People's Committee (NKPC), hence, eliminating the word "interim" and thereby establishing a "permanent-type" government, with Kim Il Sung reelected as its chairman.[75] In the reorganization that followed, *Kapsanist* Kim Ch'aek, who was concurrently serving as deputy commander of the SCGTC and commandant of the P'yŏngyang Institute, was politically appointed vice chairman of the NKPC. The new NKPC adopted many

---

* Each infantry division was organized with three rifle regiments. The 2nd Division included the 4th, 16th, and 17th Rifle Regiments.

changes, including the addition of three bureaus, two departments, and the renaming of the Security Bureau to the Internal Affairs Bureau, which was headed by *Yananist* Pak Il-u.[76] Pak, a confidant of Kim Il Sung, was the former deputy of the Korean military-political school in Yanan.[77] His leadership placed a *Yananist* in charge of North Korea's military and police for the first time.

Within two months of the opening session of the People's Assembly, a decision was made to deploy to Manchuria some thirty thousand North Korean soldiers, many of whom were raw recruits in support of the Chinese Communists' fight against Jiang Jieshi's (Chiang Kai-shek's) Nationalist Army.[78] These Korean soldiers were principally used to fill the ranks of the existing Korean Chinese divisions of the Fourth Field Army (the former Northeastern Field Army),* which most notably included the 155th, 156th, 164th, and 166th People's Liberation Army (PLA) Divisions.[79] The North Korean decision to support the Chinese Communists with manpower forged a strong bond between the two that remained throughout the years. Likewise, the battlefields in China and Manchuria served as schoolmasters to tens of thousands of Korean soldiers.

With the formation of North Korea's first elected government by the People's Assembly, the Soviets initiated their first major troop withdrawal from the peninsula in March 1947.[80] According to a U.S. Department of State report, this left only about ten thousand occupation troops remaining in Korea.[81] This major redeployment of the Red Army to the Soviet Union left a temporary void of security forces in North Korea. To mitigate this shortage, the process of creating an indigenous military continued. Begun a year earlier, the Soviet Civil Administration and the NKIPC Security Bureau had instituted a "selective recruitment" process that in essence annually drafted twenty thousand people between the ages of eighteen to twenty-two for military-type service.

While this period of "selective recruitment" continued, the Security Bureau levied draft quotas upon each province.† In turn, provinces

---

* The Fourth Field Army traces its geneaology through, in reverse order, the Northeastern Field Army, the Northeastern Allied Forces, and the Northeastern Democratic Allied Forces.
† From November 1945 to February 1947, selective recruitment was directed by the Security Bureau, which was succeeded by the Internal Affairs Bureau from February 1947 to February 1948, followed thereafter by the Ministry of National Defense.

distributed their quotas to townships and villages, which selected their recruits by using local draft boards that were composed of chairmen from the people's committee, Labor Party, and social organizations.[82] In a sparsely populated nation of less than ten million people,[83] the mobilization of manpower to expand the size of the military would have conflicted with the labor needs of industry, agriculture, and others; thus, conscription was held, at that time, to only twenty thousand people per year (doubling to forty thousand from 1949).

To command this quickly expanding armed force, the SCGTC was enhanced and redesignated the People's Army Group General Headquarters, or *Inminjipdangun Ch'ongsaryŏngbu* on 17 May 1947.[84] On that same day the previously enlarged aviation company was upgraded to a separate air force detachment and was directly subordinated as a headquarters separate from the People's Army Group General Headquarters.[85] The withdrawing Soviet army transferred vast amounts of military equipment to the North Koreans, including a modest number of aircraft, which facilitated the enlargement of the aviation company. Left behind were YAK-90 trainers, YAK fighters, IL-10 attack bombers, and reconnaissance planes.

On 26 October 1947 the Central Security Cadre School graduated its first class of officers. Kim Il Sung addressed the graduating body, congratulating students on their accomplishments and stating that they were the strength of the nation. Continuing, Kim admonished them to prepare for the task of liberating their homeland, saying: "Comrades, for the independence of the fatherland and for the benefit of the people, you must become excellent military officers who can fight to the end. We must struggle to establish a mighty people's army that, when needed, can fanatically fight to annihilate the enemies of our nation and its people."[86]

As North Korea hurried to establish an independent national government and military, the United Nations was attempting to unify the Korean peninsula under a popularly elected Korean government. To this end, in November 1947 the General Assembly of the United Nations, pursuant to Resolution 112, designated an eight-state committee, named the Temporary Commission on Korea (UNTCOK), and endowed it with the authority to oversee nationwide elections in Korea by 31 March 1948.[87] Additionally, in accordance with the same resolution, Korea's new national government was urged to "constitute its own national security forces and dissolve all military or semi-military formations."[88] In contravention to the United Nations' request, the Soviet Union responded by blocking UNTCOK from entering North Korea, which allowed the north to continue uninterrupted the task of building its own independent state.

On 6 and 7 February 1948, during the fourth session of the People's Assembly, an agreement was made to officially establish the nation's military and to subordinate it to a National Defense Bureau, or *Powiguk.* To this end, the NKPC's vice chairman, Kim Ch'aek, was temporarily appointed chief of this newly created bureau on 7 February.[89] The establishment of the National Defense Bureau signaled a separation between the roles of the military and that of the *poandae,* or police. By this time many of the provincial-level *poandae-dŭl* had evolved to assume a new role as *kyŏngbitae,* or Border Constabulary,[90] which was empowered with the responsibility of preserving the integrity of the nation's borders. Accordingly, both the *poandae* and *kyŏngbitae* remained under the control of the Internal Affairs Bureau, while the military was subordinated to the National Defense Bureau.

On the following day, in a military review in P'yŏngyang, the People's Army Group was renamed the (North) Korean People's Army. In his inauguration speech, Kim Il Sung said:

> Celebrating the second anniversary of the establishment of the North Korean People's Committee—the genuine people's power—we proclaim today the founding of the Korean People's Army, the first armed forces of the people's own in the history of Korea....
>
> After liberation, how anxiously our people longed to become, as early as possible, a proud nation with its own army! At last this long-cherished desire of the Korean people has been realized in North Korea today....
>
> The creation of the People's Army is only the first step towards building a powerful, modern military of the Democratic People's Republic of Korea, which must be established in the future.[91]

Joined with the forces of the NKPA that day were ten thousand soldiers from the Yi Hong-gwang Detachment (YHD), a *Yananist* military group that had just returned from combat duty alongside the CCF.[92]

The top leadership of the nation's newly formed military included Gen. Ch'oe Yong-gŏn, a *Kapsanist* as NKPA commander; Lt. Gen. Han Il-mu, a Soviet Korean as chief of the Naval Bureau;[93] and Lt. Gen. Kim

Won-ŭm as the air force chief. Two months before the inauguration of the NKPA, Lt. Gen. An Kil, chief of staff of the People's Army Group, had suddenly taken ill and died; as a result, 2nd NKPA Division commander Kang Kŏn was promoted to lieutenant general and elevated to this post.[94] Maj. Gen. Yi Ch'ŏng-song moved into the position Kang vacated in the 2nd NKPA Division.[95]

The formation of the NKPA signaled to the international community North Korea's determination to establish an independent state and its possession of an adequate military to protect its sovereignty. Thereafter, by late February the United Nations had abandoned its aspirations to oversee nationwide elections on the Korean peninsula and directed UNTCOK to proceed with its mission exclusively in South Korea,[96] which led to the establishment of the Republic of Korea on 15 August 1948. North Korea in turn followed suit by creating its own independent state, named the Democratic People's Republic of Korea (DPRK) on 9 September 1948.

MINISTRIES OF NATIONAL DEFENSE AND INTERNAL AFFAIRS

In the process of establishing the DPRK, a political cabinet was organized and Kim Il Sung was named premier. Although most of the bureau chiefs, who had served in the earlier North Korean administrations (FNKPAB, NKIPC, and NKPC), were not nominated to serve as cabinet ministers, such was not the case with National Defense minister Ch'oe Yong-gŏn or Internal Affairs minister Pak Il-u (see appendix C).

It should be remembered that when the National Defense Bureau was created, earlier in the year, then-vice chairman Kim Ch'aek was selected as its temporary head. With the organization of the new government, Kim Ch'aek served as vice premier, while Ch'oe Yong-gŏn, NKPA commander and former Security Bureau chief, was nominated to serve as National Defense minister. The Ministry of National Defense (MND), or *Powisŏng,* was subdivided into three types of bureaus: standard military bureaus, political bureaus, and law enforcement and control bureaus, each supervised by a vice minister of general officer rank. *Kapsanists* Ch'oe Hyŏn and Kim Il were selected for critical leadership

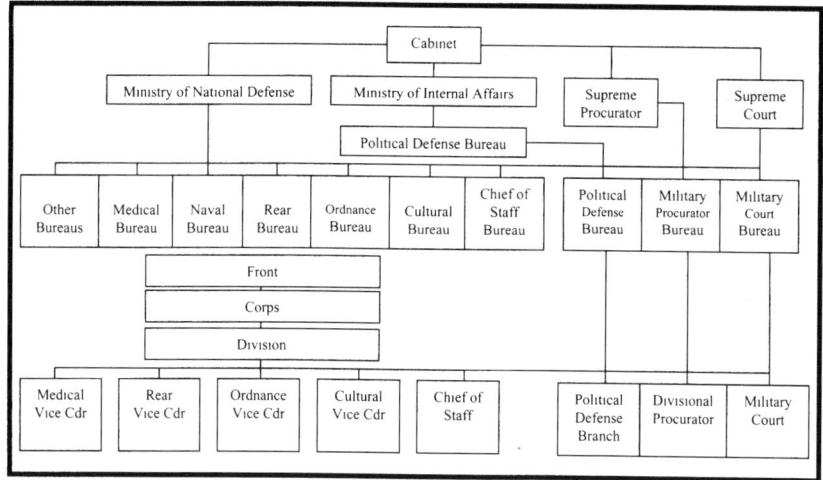

FIGURE 1. North Korea Ministry of Defense Organization Chart, June 1950
Source: U.S. Department of State, *North Korea: A Case Study in the Techniques of Take-over* (Washington, DC: U.S. Government Printing Office, 1961), 46.

positions in the political bureaus. With Kim loyalists directing political training throughout the military, any possible attempt at internal subversion was adequately mitigated. Included among the standard military bureaus was the Bureau of General Chief of Staff, which was responsible for several staff sections, including personnel, intelligence and cryptography, operations, engineering, and communications; the Artillery Command Bureau; Rear (or logistics) Bureau; Medical Bureau; Ordnance Bureau; Naval Bureau; and the Air Bureau.

In addition, the Cultural Bureau oversaw the functions of the Korean Labor Party and Youth Leagues as they applied to the military. The Political Defense Bureau was responsible for investigating crimes against the state; the Military Procurator Bureau was charged with investigating ordinary crimes and prosecuting all types of crime; and the Military Court Bureau punished all criminals. As graphically represented in figure 1, the Ministry of National Defense supervised and administered the affairs of all the military bureaus and the cultural bureau and exercised administrative authority over the Political Defense Bureau, Military Procurator Bureau, and the Military Court Bureau. Supervisory responsibility of these latter three bureaus was delegated to the Ministry of Internal Affairs, or *Naemusŏng*.[97]

Internal Affairs minister Pak Il-u supervised a massive organization; the ministry had four functional bureaus, including the Political Defense Bureau, the Security Bureau, the Defense Bureau, and the Prison Bureau. The Political Defense Bureau was an elite corps of secret police tasked with investigating cases of foreign espionage and domestic loyalty, or "thought crimes." The Security Bureau oversaw the maintenance of public order and security through the employment of some 12,000 police officers, maintaining 5 to 10 officers in the township, 40 to 50 officers in the county, 60 to 70 officers in the city, and 110 to 125 officers in the province. Additionally, a 5,000-person security guard unit was divided among the country's six provinces as a police reserve force. The Defense Bureau, as the ministry's largest bureau, had a force of 40,000 people organized into Border Constabularies, which included the Railroad Guards.[98]

Again, there are discrepancies between U.S. intelligence reports on the actual composition of the Border Constabulary brigades. Consensus is that there were forces in the north that defended the Amnok and Tumen River boundaries, forces along the 38th parallel defending the southern boundary, and another force that was dedicated to protecting the nation's railways.

According to military historian Roy Appleman, the Border Constabulary (BC) was organized into five brigades—the 1st, 2nd, 3rd, 5th, and 7th Brigades. Accordingly, the 1st, 3rd, and 7th Brigades defended along the 38th parallel, with the 7th BC Brigade defending in the west from the coast to Haeju, the 3rd Brigade in the center defending from Haeju to Ch'ŏrwŏn, and the 1st Brigade defending in the east from Ch'ŏrwŏn to the coast. Kim Ch'ang-sun refers to the southern BC brigades collectively as the *Samp'al Kyŏngbi Yŏdan,* or the 38th Constabulary Brigade (named after the 38th parallel).[99] In the north, the 2nd BC Brigade defended from coast to coast along the southern portion of the Amnok and Tumen Rivers. Headquartered in P'yŏngyang was the 5th BC Brigade, or Railroad Guards. Border Constabulary brigades were organized with six to seven battalions, and each battalion had a headquarters and a service company, three rifle companies, a machine gun and mortar company, and an antitank platoon.[100]

NKPA ORGANIZATIONAL STRUCTURE

In accordance with Kim Il Sung's stated aspiration to "build a powerful, modern military," the task continued in earnest, as the army's first tank unit—the 105th Armored Battalion—was formed in October 1948 under the command of Yu Kyŏng-su.[101] The 105th Armored Battalion had three tank companies, each equipped with four T-34 tanks; thus, including the battalion commander's tank, the 105th had thirteen tanks,* all of which had been transferred to the NKPA by the withdrawing Soviet occupation forces.[102] The T-34 tank was a medium-sized Soviet tank used extensively during World War II, and it was an outstanding combat multiplier for the NKPA. It had an 85-mm main gun, two mounted 7.62-mm machine guns, and a five-man crew.

With the growth of the military to some sixty thousand troops, the NKPA Headquarters had a need to create two more ground divisions;[103] namely, the 3rd NKPA Division, which was activated at P'yŏngyang around October 1948 and was initially commanded by Maj. Gen. Kim Kwang-hyŏp, a *Kapsanist;* and the 4th NKPA Division, located at Chinnamp'o,[104] which was commanded by Maj. Gen. Yi Chŏn-mu.[105] Following a triangular model (see below), the 3rd NKPA Division was assigned the 7th, 8th, and 9th Rifle Regiments, which were stationed on the eastern seaboard near the towns of Ch'ŏrwŏn, Wŏnsan, and Hamhŭng, respectively.[106] Reportedly, the division artillery regiment was collocated with the 8th Rifle Regiment at Wŏnsan, and from early 1949 the division headquarters was relocated to Hamhŭng.[107]

At full strength, an NKPA division was a triangular organization of 12,092 soldiers. A division had three rifle regiments, a rifle regiment had three battalions, a battalion had three companies, a company had three platoons, and a platoon had three squads. In addition, each rifle regiment had its own antitank company with four 45-mm antitank guns; one mortar company that was equipped with six 120-mm mortars, and one artillery battery that had four 76-mm howitzers. Each rifle battalion also had an organic heavy weapons company that included an antitank platoon with two 42-mm antitank guns, and one mortar platoon with nine 82-mm mortars.†

---

* Compare this to thirty-one tanks in a North Korean tank battalion today.
† An organic element is one that is assigned to and forms an essential part of a military organization.

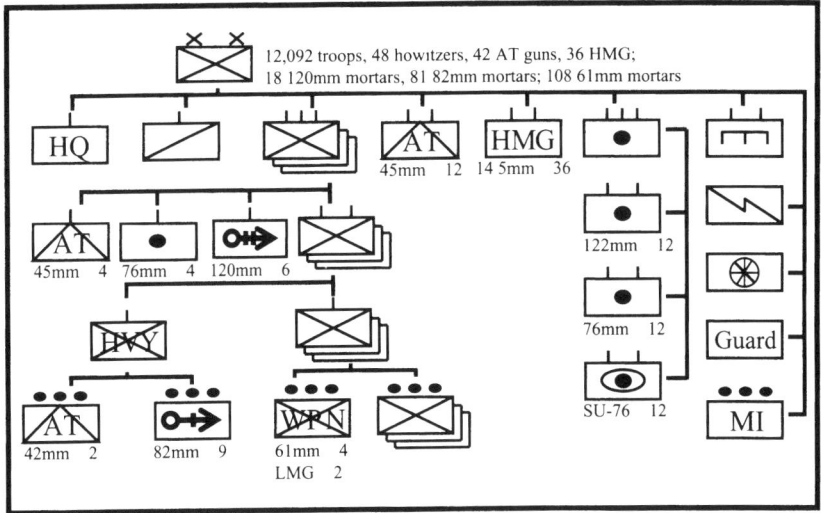

FIGURE 2. NKPA Infantry Division Organization Chart, 1950
KEY: XX = division; III = regiment; II = battalion; I = company; ••• = platoon;
AT = antitank; HMG = heavy machine gun; HQ = headquarters; HVY = heavy
weapons; WPN = weapons; double slash = infantry; lazy E = engineer; lightning
bolt = signal; circle = artillery; arrow = mortar. Source: *Hanguk chŏnjaengsa:
pochâunggyojae* (Taejŏn, Korea: Yukkun Taehak, 2001), 22.

Finally, each rifle company had its own weapons platoon, which was
equipped with four 61-mm mortars and two light machine guns.[108]

In addition to the three rifle regiments, each NKPA division was
organized with a headquarters company, a reconnaissance company, a
field artillery regiment of three artillery battalions, an antitank battalion,
a heavy machine gun battalion, an engineer battalion, a signal detachment, a transportation detachment, a guard detachment, and an intelligence platoon.[109] Each artillery battalion had three artillery batteries
that were equipped with four artillery pieces, for a total of twelve artillery pieces per battalion. Two of the battalions had towed artillery
pieces—one of those with twelve 76-mm howitzers and the other with
twelve 122-mm howitzers. The third artillery battalion was equipped
with twelve SU-76 self-propelled howitzers, each of which had a 76.2-
mm tube. Finally, the division's antitank battalion was equipped with
twelve 45-mm antitank guns, and the heavy machine gun battalion had
thirty-six 14.5-mm machine guns (see figure 2).[110]

An average NKPA division had some two hundred vehicles,[111] all
of which were necessary to maneuver and supply such a heavy force.

Appropriately, then, this Soviet-equipped army, although not as armor- or mechanized-centric as its sponsor, adopted much of the Soviets' military doctrine and tactics, incorporating combined arms operations and depending upon conventional lines of communication for resupply. Offensive maneuver, which was the NKPA's principal tactical operation, focused on frontal attacks that were supported by tanks and artillery and augmented by infantry forces conducting rear area infiltrations and en- velopments of enemy defensives. Typical of the era, such attacks were often conducted in the open and during hours of daylight. The strength of combined arms tactics is self-evident, including the ability to synchro- nize speed of maneuver with the massing of heavy firepower. These same strengths, however, have inherent vulnerabilities, including a reliance on long logistic lines, a heavy consumption of supplies, and a dependency upon established transportation corridors, which establish patterns of predictability that opposing forces can easily target, particularly with attack air and field artillery assets.

Although the type and amount of combat equipment in an NKPA division was significantly less than that of a Soviet or American division, it was appreciably more than that of a Chinese PLA division, or more importantly, that of a Republic of Korea Army (ROKA) division—its targeted opponent. A brief examination of the tactics and organizational structure of these other types of circa-1950 army divisions—namely, the Soviet, American, Chinese, and South Korean divisions—provides an appreciable understanding of the comparative capabilities of an NKPA division.

SOVIET ARMY ORGANIZATIONAL STRUCTURE

After 1945 the Soviet army demobilized from more than 500 divisions to 175 divisions, which facilitated the mechanization/motorization of the entire force.[112] Each of the Soviet first echelon divisions—armored, mechanized, and motorized—reflected the experiences of World War II, including the integration of armor, infantry, artillery, and antiaircraft at the regimental level.

In 1951 the Soviet mechanized division, which had 12,500 sol- diers, 176 medium tanks, and 54 howitzers, was further strengthened

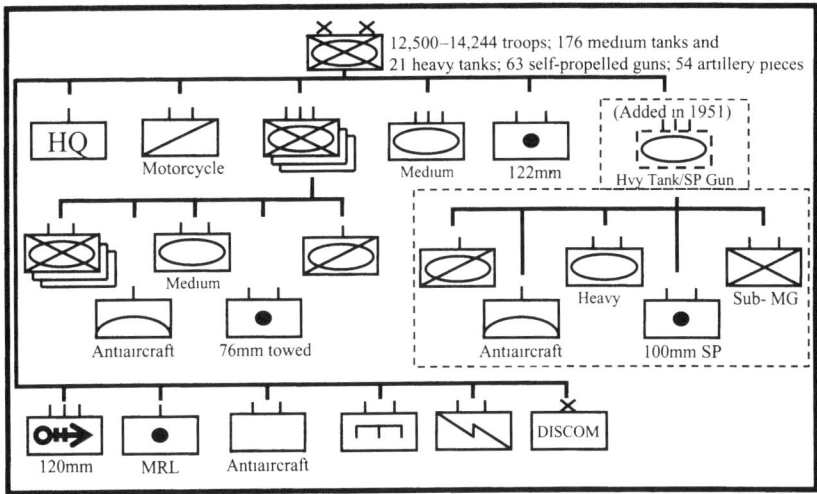

FIGURE 3. Soviet Army Mechanized Division Organization Chart, 1946–1951
KEY: XX = division; III = regiment; II = battalion; I = company; DISCOM = division support command, HQ = headquarters; MG = machine gun; MRL = multiple rocket launcher; double slash = infantry; slash = reconnaissance; oval = armor; lazy E = engineer; lightning bolt = signal; circle = artillery; arrow = mortar. Source: Jonathan M. House, *Toward Combined Arms Warfare: A Survey of 20th-Century Tactics, Doctrine, and Organization* (U.S. Army Command and General Staff College, Combat Studies Institute no. 2, 1984), 143.

by adding a heavy tank/self-propelled gun regiment to its organization of three mechanized infantry regiments, one armored regiment, one artillery regiment, and one motorcycle battalion, bringing its total combat strength to 14,244 personnel, 197 tanks, 63 self-propelled guns, and 54 howitzers. A mechanized infantry regiment had three infantry battalions, one tank battalion, one 76-mm artillery battalion, and one armored scout company. The heavy tank/self-propelled regiment had two self-propelled gun battalions, one tank battalion, one submachine gun battalion, and one armored scout company (see figure 3).[113]

In 1947 a Soviet tank division had 11,541 soldiers, 252 tanks, 84 self-propelled guns, and 24 howitzers that were principally organized into five maneuver regiments, including three medium tank regiments, one heavy tank/self-propelled gun regiment, and one motorized infantry regiment.

In a medium tank regiment there were three tank battalions, one antitank self-propelled gun battalion, one motorized infantry battalion, and

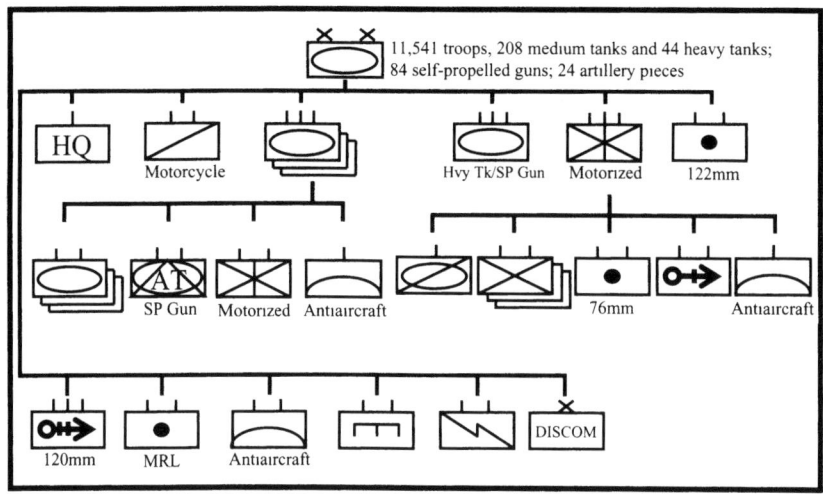

FIGURE 4. Soviet Army Tank Division Organization Chart, 1947
KEY: XX = division; III = regiment; II = battalion; I = company; AT = antitank; DISCOM = division support command; HQ = headquarters; MRL = multiple rocket launcher; double slash = infantry; slash = reconnaissance; oval = armor; lazy E = engineer; lightning bolt = signal; circle = artillery; arrow = mortar. Source: Jonathan M. House, *Toward Combined Arms Warfare: A Survey of 20th-Century Tactics, Doctrine, and Organization* (U.S. Army Command and General Staff College, Combat Studies Institute no. 2, 1984), 143.

a machine gun company. A motorized rifle regiment had three motorized rifle battalions, one 76-mm howitzer battalion, one mortar battalion, one armored scout company, and one machine gun company (see figure 4).[114]

Soviet military doctrine essentially remained unchanged until 1953, when it adopted a strategy focused on nuclear weapons, leading it to abolish its remaining rifle, mechanized, and horse cavalry divisions, and retaining only its armored, motorized rifle, and airborne rifle divisions, as they were considered more survivable on a nuclear battlefield.[115] The quintessential element of the Soviet combined arms doctrine was the frontal attack. This tactic was conducted in phases and began as company- and battalion-sized units conducted reconnaissance by fire maneuvers to neutralize the forward security elements of their opposing forces and to identify the location and composition of the enemy's main defenses.

The Soviet army initiated the main attack by massing artillery, tank, and direct-fire weapons against a small portion of a defender's perimeter, creating a penetration just large enough to encircle and defeat its enemy. After creating a breach in the enemy's defenses, follow-on forces would assault through the breach in order to encircle and destroy the defender. Completing the encirclement, an exploitation and pursuit force continued the attack deep into its opponent's rear, eventually halting at its objective in order to consolidate its forces and to establish a hasty defense before reaching the point of tactical culmination. A combined arms organization, called a forward detachment, conducted the exploitation (which set the conditions for the follow-on offensive attack), employing mobility and firepower to seize key objectives and to disrupt its opponent's attempts to reorganize the defense. Typically, a forward detachment, operating as much as ninety kilometers forward of the main element, was organized around a tank brigade that was reinforced by batteries of field artillery, antiaircraft artillery, engineers, and close air support.

UNITED STATES ARMY ORGANIZATIONAL STRUCTURE

In 1945 and 1946 the U.S. War Department conducted an extensive review of past organizations and future mission requirements to determine how to properly organize for future combat. Lessons learned indicated that the United States' triangular infantry division of World War II was woefully inadequate, lacking sufficient combat strength and necessary organic support assets. This previously used triangular infantry division involved 15,245 soldiers, 48 howitzers, and 68 antitank guns primarily organized into three infantry regiments, of three battalions each, and one artillery regiment, of three 105-mm artillery battalions and one 155-mm artillery battalion. By November 1946 the War Department authorized a variety of changes to the infantry division, including increasing its end strength to 17,700 soldiers, 141 tanks, and 72 howitzers. Additionally, the division received an authorization for an antiaircraft machine gun battalion, a 4.2-inch mortar company organic to each of the three infantry regiments, and the addition of recoilless rifles for each infantry battalion. Organizational changes also reduced the infantry squad from twelve to nine men (see figure 5).[116]

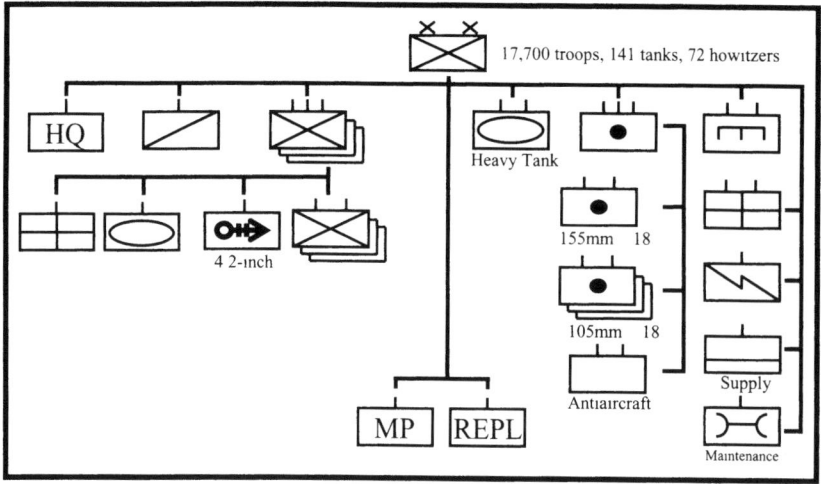

FIGURE 5. U.S. Army Infantry Division Organization Chart, 1947
KEY: XX = division; III = regiment; II = battalion; I = company; HQ =
headquarters; MP = military police; REPL = personnel replacement; double slash =
infantry; slash = reconnaissance; oval = armor; lazy E = engineer; lightning bolt =
signal; circle = artillery; arrow = mortar; cross = medical.
Source: Jonathan M. House, *Toward Combined Arms Warfare: A Survey of*
20th-Century Tactics, Doctrine, and Organization (U.S. Army Command and General
Staff College, Combat Studies Institute no. 2, 1984), 148.

Similarly, organizational changes occurred in the United States' armored division, including increasing the division's mechanized infantry
force from three battalions of three companies to four battalions of four
companies. In addition, the armored division received an authorization
for one 155-mm self-propelled artillery battalion, one antiaircraft machine gun battalion, a fourth engineer line company, a bridge company,
and a substantial increase of wheeled vehicles, including a near-doubling
of two-and-a-half-ton cargo trucks (from 422 to 804 trucks). In total, the
United States' armored division of 1947 was authorized 14,975 soldiers,
361 tanks, and 72 self-propelled howitzers (see figure 6).[117]

Most of these organizational changes, however, were never imple-
mented, as the United States Army drastically contracted in size and
became little more than a garrison force, occupying Germany and Japan
with hollowed-out forces in the United States. By 1950, with the exception of one division in Germany, the United States Army had yet to equip
any of its divisions, even remotely, in accordance with its authorized table

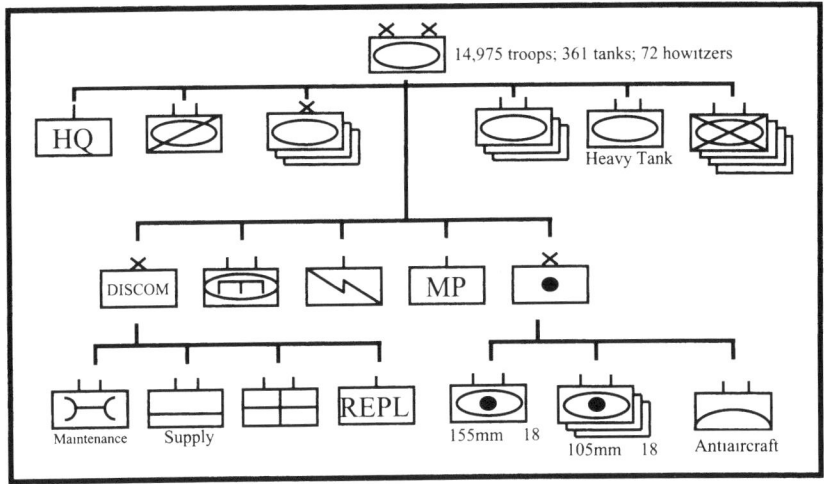

FIGURE 6. U.S. Army Armored Division Organization Chart, 1947
KEY: XX = division; X = brigade; II = battalion; I = company; DISCOM = division support command; HQ = headquarters; MP = military police; REPL = personnel replacement; double slash = infantry; slash = reconnaissance; oval = armor; lazy E = engineer; lightning bolt = signal; circle = artillery; cross = medical.
Source: Jonathan M. House, *Toward Combined Arms Warfare: A Survey of 20th-Century Tactics, Doctrine, and Organization* (U.S. Army Command and General Staff College, Combat Studies Institute no. 2, 1984), 148.

of organization and equipment (TO&E). In 1950 the four U.S. divisions in Japan possessed only two-thirds of their authorized personnel and equipment, including only two of three infantry battalions per infantry regiment, only one of six tank companies, one of three antiaircraft batteries, and only two of three 105-mm field artillery batteries per battalion.[118]

These de facto organizational shortages left the army with a force structure that was inconsistent with its combined arms doctrine. In essence, infantry regiments maneuvered as pure units with reduced artillery support and with no augmentation of tanks. Consequently, deprived of their primary antitank weapon—the tank—regimental infantry commanders had to resort to using the obsolete 2.36-inch rocket launcher. Equally detrimental to combat operations, if not more so, was the effect of having only two maneuver battalions in a regiment, which prohibited a regiment from employing a reserve force and increased the dispersion and isolation of defending units, particularly in mountainous terrain like that found in Korea.

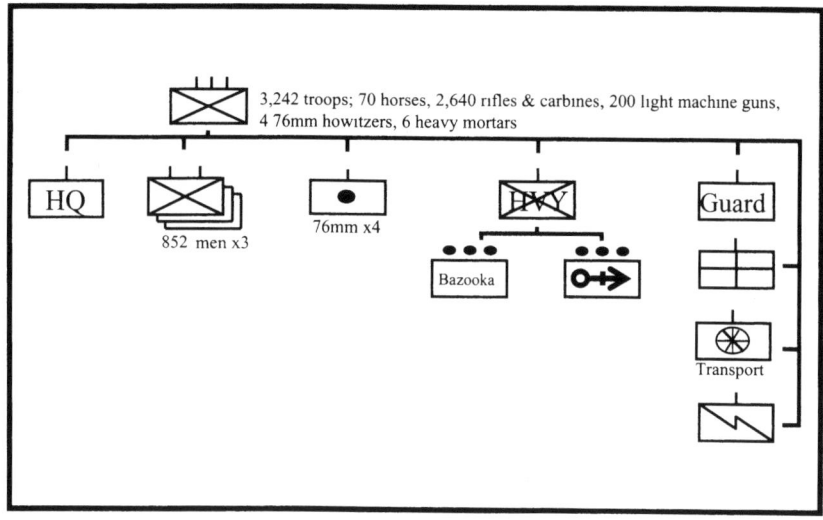

FIGURE 7. PLA Infantry Regiment Organization Chart, 1950
KEY: III = regiment; II = battalion; I = company; ••• = platoon; HQ = headquarters; HVY = heavy weapons; double slash = infantry; cross = medical; lightning bolt = signal; circle = artillery; arrow = mortar.
Source: Robert B. Rigg, *Red China's Fighting* Hordes (Harrisburg, PA: Military Service Publishing Company, 1951), 65.

PLA ORGANIZATIONAL STRUCTURE

Unlike the infantry divisions of the Soviets, Americans, South Koreans, or North Koreans, the Chinese People's Liberation Army of 1950 was a different type of army, organized to leverage its weaknesses and to exploit its unique strengths. With a force structure of about twelve thousand soldiers,[119] a PLA infantry division was lightly equipped, with only twelve 76-mm howitzers (an NKPA division had forty-eight, including twelve medium-caliber guns), eighteen heavy mortars, nine heavy machine guns (an NKPA division had thirty-six guns), no trucks (an NKPA division had 200 trucks), and fewer antitank weapons than an NKPA division possessed (see figure 7).[120]

Armies whose main focus is on heavy equipment require large support organizations that are capable of repairing and replacing equipment, as well as providing a robust flow of supplies (including large-caliber munitions, fuel, lubricants, replacement vehicles, and spare parts) over great distances. During the 1940s the PLA had limited access to this type of equipment and logistical support.[121] In fact, the combat equipment that the army did possess was primarily a hodgepodge of individual and crew-served weapons that the PLA acquired during the anti-Japanese war and the Chinese civil war. Some units were armed with Soviet-made weapons, and other units had Japanese-made weapons, but the majority of the PLA divisions were armed with American-made weapons that had been captured from the U.S.-backed nationalist Chinese during that country's civil war.[122] Not until 1950 did the PLA begin to standardize its weapons type,[123] which it accomplished by conducting whole-scale arms purchases from the Soviet Union. Neither did the PLA have the capability to protect vulnerable logistic lines against a formidable opponent like the United States. Therefore, by amplifying its inherent strength—manpower—the PLA organized its forces into light infantry units that were trained in mobile, positional, and guerrilla warfare tactics, including infiltrating, probing, feinting, and withdrawing. Since PLA tactics obviated the army's reliance on the use of air, artillery, and armored support, its forces were able to move undetected off roads and through difficult terrain while it maximized concealment under the cover of darkness and inclement weather. Additionally, the PLA avoided the habitual use of supply trains by either carrying its supplies or subsisting off the land.

Unlike conventional forces, which typically fought during the hours of daylight, the PLA attacked mostly at night, engaging its opponent from the rear and at close range with large quantities of light munitions, including hand grenades, light machine guns, and man-packed mortars. In developing the PLA doctrine, Mao Zedong followed closely the maxims of Sun Tzu: "All warfare is based on deception. Therefore, when capable, feign incapacity; when active, inactivity. When near, make it appear that you are far away; when far away, that you are near. Offer the enemy a bait to lure him; feign disorder and strike him. When he concentrates, prepare against him; where he is strong avoid him. Pretend inferiority and encourage his arrogance. Keep him under a strain and wear him down. Attack where he is unprepared; sally out when he does not expect you."[124]

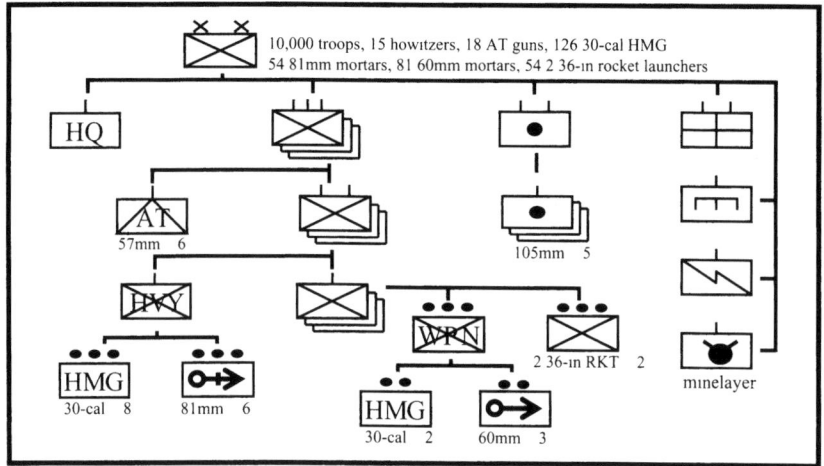

FIGURE 8. ROKA Infantry Division Organization Chart, 1950
KEY: XX = division; III = regiment; II = battalion; I = company; ••• = platoon;
•• = section; AT = antitank; HMG = heavy machine gun; HQ = headquarters;
HVY = heavy weapons; RKT = rocket launcher; WPN = weapons; double slash =
infantry; cross = medical; lazy E = engineer; lightning bolt = signal; circle =
artillery; arrow = mortar.
Source: Hanguk chŏnjaengsa: poch'unggyojae(Taejŏn, Korea: Yukkun Taehak,
2001), 22.

ROKA ORGANIZATIONAL STRUCTURE

By June 1950 the Republic of Korea Army had ninety-eight thousand soldiers (less than half the total of the NKPA), composed of approximately
sixty-five thousand combat troops and thirty-three thousand support personnel, who were organized into eight infantry divisions and two independent infantry regiments.[125] Similar to an NKPA infantry division,
a ROKA infantry division was organized as a triangular division that
was composed of three rifle regiments; however, personnel shortages
left three of the eight divisions undermanned, with only two regiments
each. A ROKA division was authorized ten thousand personnel, nearly
three thousand soldiers fewer than an NKPA division, which translates
to a reduction in strength of 17 percent.[126]

A ROKA rifle regiment had three rifle battalions and a 57-mm
antitank company. A rifle battalion had three rifle companies and a heavy
weapons company that was equipped with eight .30-caliber machine
guns and six 81-mm mortars. A rifle company had three rifle platoons

armed with M-1 rifles; a weapons platoon that was equipped with two .30-caliber machine guns and three 60-mm mortars; and a 2.36-inch rocket launcher platoon. In addition to the three rifle regiments of a standard ROKA division, its organic organization included a 105-mm artillery battalion that was equipped with fifteen M-3 howitzers,[127] a medical battalion, an engineer company, a mine-laying company, a signal company, and a headquarters company (see figure 8).[128]

In June 1950 the ROK Air Force had 1,865 airmen organized in a single flight group of twelve liaison-type aircraft and ten advanced trainers (AT6). Additionally, the ROK Navy/Coast Guard had 6,145 sailors who operated a small fleet of one patrol craft (PC701), one landing ship tank (LST), fifteen minesweepers, ten minelayers, and various other small crafts.[129]

Noticeably absent from the ROKA was any heavy armament, including tanks, medium artillery, 4.2-inch mortars, and recoilless rifles; neither did the ROK Air Force have any combat aircraft. Supplies were also quite limited, including only a small amount of ammunition and virtually no supply of spare parts.[130] Therefore, while the ROKA was organized and trained for conventional warfare, it lacked any significant offensive capability, and its defensive capability was quite diminutive against the rising strength of its principal adversary—the NKPA.

ORDER OF THE KOREAN NATIONAL FLAG
(Chosŏn Kukki Hunjang)
Established 12 October 1948

This award is fashioned as a 60-mm-diameter five-point shield of long silver rays. Positioned on top of the five-point shield is a five-point star of long gold rays with a cluster of three balls at the end of each point. At the center of the gold star are two concentric decagons, the outer one blue and the inner one red. Inside the red decagon is a silver circle around a gold star that is outlined in blue. On the obverse is written *Chosŏn Kukki Hunjang* (Order of the Korean National Flag), and depending on the award, either *che 1 kŭp* (1st class) or *che 2 kŭp* (2nd class). The 1st class order has a neck bandage and the 2nd class order has a pin back. (Art by Matthew S. Minnich)

• 3 •

Expansion of the (North) Korean People's Army: Chinese Communist Influences

SOVIET WITHDRAWAL

THE YEAR 1948 ended with the Red Army removing its last two infantry divisions from the Korean peninsula on 26 December, officially ending the Soviet military occupation of North Korea.[1] In its place the Soviets established a diplomatic mission to North Korea in January 1949, where according to United States intelligence, the Soviets continued to instruct the North Korean government as they deemed appropriate.[2]

In a matter of three years the Soviets and North Koreans had created a well-trained and equipped national defense force totaling some one hundred thousand personnel, including four infantry divisions, a forty-thousand-man BC force, and a tank battalion. In the eighteen months that followed the final Soviet withdrawal from the Korean peninsula, this defense force doubled in size to include a total of ten infantry divisions, one armored division, one air division, and an increasingly larger naval force. Although much of the NKPA's continued growth is properly attributed to continued Soviet efforts—particularly the transfer of combat equipment—a large percentage of military manpower actually arrived from Communist China in the form of deactivated PLA infantry divisions. This infusion of PLA-trained military manpower into the NKPA was an initial catalyst that led to its increased adoption of elements of Mao Zedong's military doctrine, which had been learned by Koreans who had fought in Manchuria and China during the 1930s and 1940s.[3]

Principles of Chinese Communist military doctrine, as developed over many years of semi-guerrilla warfare, were based on the concept of a protracted war. Under this doctrine, war was fought in three phases, based on the advantages of asymmetry that were made necessary by the technological and logistical inferiority of Mao's Red Army. Consistent in all three phases of this doctrine is the employment of guerrilla forces. In the first phase, guerrilla forces fight harassing battles in the enemy's rear area, while conventional forces defend against the enemy's offensive attacks. The second phase is marked by a period of stalemate, whereby neither conventional force is capable of overmatching its opponent; it is during this phase that the guerrilla war assumes preeminence. In phase 3 the conventional force transitions to the offense and attacks its defending opponent, while guerrilla forces assist by attacking the opponent's logistic bases.[4] Although this doctrine was understood and adopted in a very limited form, it was not until after the Korean War that the NKPA embraced it as a central aspect of its military strategy, referring to it as its mixed tactics strategy, or *paehap chŏllyak*.[5]

This chapter briefly examines the growth of the NKPA from late 1948 until the commencement of the Korean War, just eighteen months later, on 25 June 1950.

THE (NORTH) KOREAN PEOPLE'S ARMY'S RAPID EXPANSION

In late 1948, as the Chinese Communist Forces destroyed the Chinese Nationalist Forces in Manchuria, the Chinese civil war shifted from Manchuria to China proper.[6] As a result, the CCF transferred tens of thousands of ethnic-Korean soldiers (most of whom originated from Manchuria) to North Korea throughout the months that followed. Consequently, in 1949 the NKPA grew to a force of over 120,000 men, including some 40,000 new conscripts. Such a massive increase in the levying of conscript soldiers required draft boards to rely on coercion in order to achieve their quotas.[7] Additionally, 30,000 to 40,000 ethnic-Korean soldiers were transferred from the PLA's Fourth Field Army to the NKPA.[8] Included in this count were troops from the 164th and 166th PLA Divisions (former KVA divisions), which crossed the Amnok River by rail to the towns of Nanam and Manp'ojin, respectively, in July 1949.[9] According to a U.S. Department of State report, once these units arrived in Korea, they exchanged their commandeered U.S. military equipment for Soviet-built equipment. Men from these two units were then used to activate the 5th and 6th NKPA Divisions.[10]

Accordingly, 7,500 soldiers of the 164th PLA Division were re-organized into the 10th, 11th, and 12th Rifle Regiments of the 5th NKPA Division, under the command of Maj. Gen. Kim Ch'ang-dŏk—a *Yananist*.[11] Likewise, ten thousand men of the 166th PLA Division were used to form the 13th, 14th, and 15th Rifle Regiments of the 6th NKPA Division.[12] As both divisions were filled to authorized strength, it is likely that domestic-trained conscripts (or natives) were used to bring each unit to full strength. Selected to command the 6th NKPA Division was Maj. Gen. Pang Ho-san, who, like the 5th NKPA Division commander, was a *Yananist*.[13] Pang Ho-san had begun his military career years earlier as a cadet at Huangpu (Whampoa) Military Academy in Guangzhou (Canton), China.[14] He later instructed at a Yanan military school before joining the YHD, where he served as commander of the 166th PLA Division.

That same year some ten thousand NKPA troops returned from an extended training program in Siberia. These soldiers—who had been trained in air and armor combat techniques—returned to Korea, facilitating the expansion of the NKPA air detachment into an air division, and the 105th NKPA Armored Battalion into an armored regiment in May 1949.[15] Other soldiers became military instructors and taught courses at the NKPA Armor and Ordnance Schools. In addition, that year the Coast Guard Corps, which had previously been controlled by the Ministry of Internal Affairs, was transferred to the Naval Bureau of the Ministry of National Defense on 20 August 1949. Nine days later, the navy activated its first torpedo unit.[16]

In January 1950 Premier Kim Il Sung dispatched Maj. Gen. Kim Kwang-hyŏp, 3rd NKPA Division commander, to China to seek the release of all ethnic-Korean soldiers who were then serving in the PLA's Fourth Field Army.[17] Most of these soldiers were Korean residents in China who had joined the Chinese army in Northeast China during the last stage of the anti-Japanese war and the Chinese civil war.[18] Kim Kwang-hyŏp requested that these soldiers be permitted to bring their arms and military equipment with them, stating: "The Korean army does not have extra weapons and equipment. We have to approach the Soviet Union again for weapons' purchases, after we incorporate those fourteen thousand soldiers into our army. The communication and negotiations will take a long time. Please consider whether the Chinese comrades can equip those troops."[19]

At the behest of Marshal Nie Rongzhen, acting PLA general chief of staff, the CCP Central Committee approved this request on 22 January 1950. According to Marshal Nie Rongzhen, fourteen thousand ethnic-Korean PLA soldiers with military equipment were transferred to the NKPA, arriving in Korea in the spring of 1950.[20] However, other sources argue that in fact many more than fourteen thousand soldiers arrived from China during that period. Conversations between Professor Chen Jian of Southern Illinois University and Beijing military researchers have suggested that twenty-three thousand ethnic-Korean soldiers transferred from divisions of the PLA's 4th Field Army to Korea in the spring of 1950.[21] Furthermore, Professor Cumings's research of U.S. military intelligence records indicates that twice that many, or forty thousand to fifty thousand ethnic-Korean soldiers arrived in Korea between February and March of 1950. Specifically, it is believed that in February 1950, men from the 139th, 140th, 141st, 155th, and 156th PLA Divisions arrived in Korea and were organized into the 1st, 2nd, and 3rd Rifle Regiments of the 7th NKPA Division, which was commanded by Maj. Gen. Chŏn U.[22] In March 1950, elements from the 167th, 169th, 170th, and 171st PLA Divisions arrived in Korea to form the 25th, 27th, and 29th Rifle Regiments of the 10th NKPA Division,[23] under the command of Maj. Gen. Kim T'ae-gŭn.[24]

In March 1950, in addition to activating the 10th NKPA Division with CCF-trained soldiers, the 15th NKPA Division, commanded by Maj. Gen. Pak Sŏng-ch'ŏl, was also activated using domestic recruits.[25] The tenth, and final, division to be activated before the start of the Korean War was the 13th NKPA Division, which was formed in early June 1950 and commanded by Maj. Gen. Ch'oe Yong-jin, *a Kapsanist*.[26]

Agreements between the Chinese and the Soviets facilitated the transfer of Soviet military equipment to the NKPA by rail through Manchuria, crossing into the northwest at the border cities of Dandong, Manchuria, and Sinŭiju, Korea, and in the northeast at the border cities of Tumen, Manchuria, and Namyang, Korea.[27] Among such shipments in April and May 1950 were the heavy deliveries of tanks, tracks, and artillery systems.[28]

With the addition of that new shipment of tanks, the NKPA then had 150 T-34 tanks in its inventory. The majority of these were used to expand the 105th Armored Regiment into an armored brigade, with an increased strength of six thousand soldiers and 120 tanks. The 105th Armored Brigade's subordinate elements included the 107th, 109th, and the 203rd Armored Regiments, each with 40 tanks, and the 206th Mechanized Infantry Regiment, which had a strength of about twenty-five hundred men.[29] In addition, an independent tank regiment, under the command of Kim Ch'ŏl-u,[30] was created with about 30 tanks and attached to the 7th NKPA Division in June 1950.

By mid-1950, following the Soviet military model, the army expanded its command structure by adding three new levels above the division; namely, the corps headquarters, the front headquarters, and at the top, a seven-man military committee composed of cabinet officials, which directed military operations.[31] In accordance with this expanded command structure, Gen. Kim Ch'aek was designated front commander, with Lt. Gen. Kang Kŏn as chief of staff.[32] Maj. Gen. Kim Ŭng, commander of the 1st NKPA, was promoted to lieutenant general and given command of the newly created I Corps on 10 June 1950. Consequently, Ch'oe Kwang, who was serving as the chief of staff for the 1st NKPA Division, was promoted to major general and assigned as the division's commander.[33] Kim Kwang-hyŏp was promoted to lieutenant general and assigned as II Corps commander on 12 June 1950.[34] Maj. Gen. Yi Yŏng-ho was then selected to assume command of the 3rd NKPA Division.[35]

The precise number of soldiers in the NKPA at the start of the Korean War has often been miscalculated over the years. U.S. intelligence reports of September and November 1950 estimated the NKPA's total strength at about 95,000 personnel.[36] However, during this same reporting period, in October 1950, researchers from the U.S. Department of State traveled to North Korea and conducted a survey of the North Korean regime. The results of the survey revealed that by early 1950 the NKPA had expanded to about 150,000 to 180,000 soldiers, plus an additional 40,000 personnel in the BC and Railroad Guards of the Ministry of Internal Affairs.[37] These latter numbers are more consistent with the figures that Kim Ch'ang-sun provides; namely, that in June 1950 the total ground force numbered 200,000, including ten infantry divisions, one tank division,[38] one air division, one motorcycle regiment, and some 40,000 personnel in the BC and Railroad Guards of the Ministry of Internal Affairs.[39] Clearly, by mid-1950 the NKPA had become offensive-capable, having fielded a combat force that was quantitatively larger (by at least a factor of two) and qualitatively better equipped than the ROKA—its principal adversary.

ORDER OF THE SOLDIER'S HONOR
(Chŏnsa ŭi Yŏngye Hunjang)

Established 1 July 1950

The Order of the Soldier's Honor was awarded for distinguished meritorious service in the war for unification, freedom, and the independence of the Fatherland. The award is fashioned as a 50-mm-diameter ten-point shield of long silver rays. Positioned on top of the ten-point shield is a crossed sword and rifle. On top of that is a five-point red star. On top of that is laid a gold shield flanked by a laurel wreath, and on top of that is a silver shield with a soldier in the center. On the obverse is written *Chŏnsa ŭi Yŏngye Hunjang* (Order of the Soldier's Honor), and depending on the class of the award, either *che 1 kŭp* (1st class) or *che 2 kŭp* (2nd class), with a pin back. (Art by Matthew S. Minnich)

• 4 •

The North Korean People's Army of 1950

FROM THE FORCED dissolution of Korea's military in 1907 until the nation's joyful liberation in 1945, Korea's few remaining active warriors had either joined with an anti-Japanese guerrilla group, which operated predominantly in China, Manchuria, and Siberia, or they had merged with one of these foreign militaries. Many of the ethnic-Korean soldiers who eventually returned to Korea with the Soviet occupation army—*Kapsanists* and Soviet Koreans—later worked with the Soviets to create the new Communist state of North Korea. As the Soviets raised Kim Il Sung to the office of national leader, Kim Il Sung concurrently exalted his small group of *Kapsanists* to key positions of power, including the nation's top military billets. These actions assisted in imprinting upon the NKPA the *Kapsan* Partisan heritage, which was exploited by the *Kapsanists* as an endorsement of their right to leadership.

Natives and *Yananists,** the other two political groups that emerged in North Korea after its liberation, contributed the greatest number of men to the NKPA—the former as individual conscripts, and the latter

---

* Although not discussed in this book, Kwak Tong-sŏ, Pak Hyo-sam, Yi ho, Han Kyŏng, O Hak-yong, Ch'i Pyŏng-hak, Ch'oe A-rip, Yi Ik-sŏng, and Ch'oe Kwang were other well-known *Yananist* NKPA leaders.

principally as collective units arriving from China. By June 1950, more than two hundred thousand North Koreans had been mustered and trained as soldiers in the nation's new military, of whom more than half were KVA veterans.[1] The type training these soldiers received was based on their point of integration. Those soldiers who fought in China and Manchuria received military training that was heavily imbued with the Chinese Communist military model, while the soldiers who trained at one of North Korea's training sites or who received specialized training in Siberia were educated in Soviet military doctrine.

The ubiquity of Soviet military advisors throughout the NKPA facilitated the rapid transformation of this fledgling military unit into a modern and capable armed force. Several field grade and general officer Soviet advisors were attached to the Ministry of National Defense. In each military academy and training center, Soviet officers supervised the training program and in some cases served as instructors; and although Soviet advisors were also integrated throughout the tactical force—from division to company level—the density of these augmentations appreciably decreased over time. In 1948, there were 150 advisors attached to North Korea's four NKPA divisions. In 1949, the number of advisors was drastically reduced to 20 per division, of which the NKPA then had six divisions. By mid-1950 there were ten divisions in the NKPA, and only 3 to 8 advisors per division.[2] This successive decrease in military advisors is indicative of the NKPA's professional growth.

The Soviets did more than just organize and instruct the NKPA; they also armed it, providing the NKPA with everything from individual fighting equipment to major weapons systems. By 1950 the NKPA's major weapons systems included a composite of five hundred T-34 tanks and SU-76 self-propelled howitzers; nearly two hundred aircraft, including one hundred YAK-type aircraft, seventy IL-10 attack bombers, and eight reconnaissance planes; and about thirty naval craft of various types.[3] The NKPA augmented its Soviet-equipped military with discarded Japanese supplies; commandeered U.S. arms, which had been captured from the Guomindang military; and weapons from its own indigenous factories, which produced 82-mm and 120-mm mortars, light machine guns, and ammunition of all types, including artillery, mortar, and small arms.[4]

In nearly sixty years since its founding, the NKPA has greatly increased in size and capability, and yet the roots of its origin—its partisan history, Soviet tutelage, and Chinese Communist influences—still help to define it today. However, no single experience accurately characterizes the nature of the NKPA. Rather, the NKPA has incorporated these and other experiences in the development of its own unique military doctrine, strategy, and force structure.

Part 2

Current Tactics

ORDER OF LABOR (Noryŏk Hunjang)
Established 17 July 1951

The Order of Labor is fashioned as a 60-mm-diameter ten-point shield of long gold rays. In the center is a five-point gold star with a hammer and sickle at its center. At the top of the star is a part of a mechanical gear, and underneath the star is an open book. A laurel wreath flanks the star. On the top of the shield is a red banner and *Noryŏk* written in gold. On the obverse is written *Chosŏn Noryŏk Hunjang* (Korea Order of Labor) and the issue number, with a pin back. (Art by Matthew S. Minnich)

• 5 •

National Strategy and Military Policy Foundation/
북한 대남전략 및 군사정책/北韓 對南戰略 및 軍事政策

ON 24 JUNE 1950, the day before the NKPA invaded South Korea, Kim Il Sung had undoubtedly assessed that his force was adequately sized, trained, and equipped to defeat the South Korean Army, and in fact, history shows that had the United States not intervened, success for the NKPA would have been virtually assured.[1] However, the United States did intervene, and by September 1950 the NKPA began to suffer great setbacks in its strategy. Consequently, on 21 December 1950 in Chakang-do, Pyŏro-ri, the NKPA held a three-day conference to critique its combat performance during the preceding six months. Many critical defects about the state of the army were addressed in those meetings. Chief among the findings were the determinations that (1) the NKPA's infantry-centric organization was unsuited to the Soviet's armored/mechanized infantry doctrine (attributed by the NKPA as the primary cause of its failures); (2) its strategic plan was inadequately developed to destroy its opponent; (3) its cadre was poorly trained in military doctrine and tactics; (4) its reserve forces were sparsely fielded; and (5) its logistical system was insufficient to supply the army's needs.[2] By the war's end neither opponent was victorious, as the fighting ceased in July 1953 with both forces located close to where they had been positioned in the summer of 1950; namely, along the 38th parallel.

MILITARY IDEOLOGY/군사사상/軍事思想

This method of analyzing combat operations was hardly episodic. Rather, it developed into North Korea's process for refining its military ideology, or *kunsa sasang,* which was originally based on Kim Il Sung's partisan experiences. In turn, North Korea's military ideology now supports and defines its national objective, military policy, military strategy, principles of war, and battlefield tactical doctrine (see figure 9). Included below are some of the lessons learned from North Korea's analyses of various global conflicts that have contributed to the nation's evolving military ideology.

As mentioned, during the Korean War, North Korea suffered from three weaknesses: a shortage of reserve forces; leaders who were in-adequately versed in strategy and tactics; and operational and tactical inefficacy. To compensate for these noted shortcomings, North Korea has presently amassed a reserve force of some 7.7 million personnel and

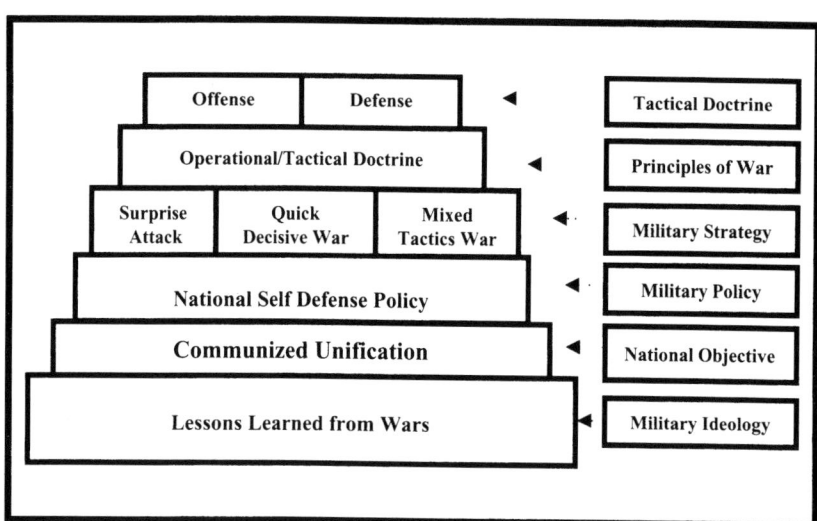

FIGURE 9. DPRK National Strategy and Military Policy Foundation Paradigm
Source: *Chŏk ŭl alcha (I): yŏndaegŭp isang pukkoegun chŏnsulgyori* (Seoul: Korean Army Headquarters, 2000), 11–17.

established a military training base that has since produced a competent and capable force.[3]

The Soviet acquiescence before the United States during the Cuban Missile Crisis of 1962, greatly eroded North Korea's confidence in its principal ally. Seeing the Kremlin capitulate on an issue of national interest and integrity engendered little hope that it would stand stalwart in the defense of North Korea. Kim Il Sung's policy of *chuch'e,* or self-reliance, thus took on an immediate sense of urgency. Within two years the government published a military guideline that outlined a process designed to develop a militarily self-reliant nation.

Lessons learned from the Vietnam War and the Arab-Israeli war of the late 1960s served as the foundation for the establishment of the NKPA's three-pillared military strategy—surprise attack, quick decisive war, and mixed tactics. In 1967 the Israelis launched a surprise attack against the country's Arab neighbors, and within six days Israel's combined armored and mechanized forces quickly maneuvered throughout the depths of the battlefield, securing a quick and decisive victory. Following this war, the NKPA mimed this strategy by greatly increasing the mechanized capability of its own armed forces. Today North Korea bases its strategy to win a quick, decisive war on its ability to launch a surprise attack and to maintain momentum by employing its one armored and four mechanized corps.

During the Vietnam War, North Vietnam was able to successfully counter a technologically superior force, in large part through the use of special operation forces (SOF). In addition, the effective use of psychological operations by the North Vietnamese vastly complicated the South Vietnamese war effort. Following this example, North Korea has since amassed approximately 120,000 SOF troops,[4] which when employed in concert with its conventional forces creates an employment concept called mixed tactics.*

After analyzing the 1991 Gulf War, the NKPA surmised that it takes the United States a significant amount of time to deploy its military forces. The NKPA study also determined that it is both difficult and

---

* During combat operations, NKPA SOF troops would likely be infiltrated into the forward and rear ROKA areas, where they would attempt to destroy C2 facilities, sever lines of communications, assassinate key leaders, and demolish or cripple major facilities such as airfields.

time-consuming for the United States to rally international support during a crisis. Additionally, the precision with which the United States military was able to detect and destroy the Iraqi army in the opening months of 1991 reconfirmed the NKPA's perceived necessity to assemble military equipment and personnel in underground facilities in order to protect them from air and ground attacks. Accordingly, after the Gulf War, North Korea increased its construction of underground facilities to the point where today it possesses as many as ten thousand such facilities.

The 1999 Kosovo War provided North Korea with an opportunity to evaluate United States military operations in an area with terrain and weather similar to that of the Korean peninsula. Likewise, NKPA analysts were able to study the adverse effects that this terrain and weather had upon America's high-tech arsenal. Washington's reluctance to commit ground troops suggested that the United States might similarly choose to employ its high-tech arsenal of cruise missiles, precision bombs, and jet fighters on a future Korean battlefield rather than risk losing American lives in ground combat. This line of analysis has prompted North Korea to consider developing methods to avoid and survive air strikes, including cyber-warfare, which would be directed at disrupting satellites, the Internet, and radio waves.

NATIONAL OBJECTIVE/국가목표/國家目標

Although North Korea failed to unify the Korean peninsula under its banner from 1950 to 1953, the country has by no means abandoned this aim. Rather, as is clearly stated in its constitution and Workers' Party Pact,* its national objective, or *kukka mokp'yo,* is to bring about the Communization of the Republic of Korea in order to establish a Communist society on the Korean peninsula.

To further underscore its national objective, in April 1965 the North Korean Central Committee announced its proposal for a three-tiered

---

* Excerpt from the *Pukchosŏn Nodongdang* (Korean Workers' Party) Pact: "The immediate goal of the *Pukchosŏn Nodongdang* is achieving a complete victory of socialism in the northern half of the republic, thereby successfully accomplishing its revolutionary mission of liberating the Korean people and establishing a people's democracy. The ultimate goal of the party is to spread *chuch'e sasang* [self-reliance thought] and construct a communist society throughout the world."

revolution. The first revolution advocated a transformation of the nation's military might. The second revolution called for the erosion of South Korea's foreign military alliance, particularly targeting the removal of United States forces and its nuclear weapons from South Korea. The final revolution, the diplomacy-turning strategy, was intended to align North Korea with a number of foreign countries while internationally isolating South Korea.

MILITARY POLICY/군사정책/軍事政策

In December 1962, at the Fifth Plenum of the Fourth NKWP Central Committee, a Four-Point Military Guideline, or *sadae kunsanosŏn*, of the National Defense Policy was adopted.* Through the implementation of these four strategies, the government's intention was to create a military force that is capable of achieving its national objective—the Communization of the Korean peninsula.

Adopted forty-three years ago, the Four-Point Military Guideline continues to serve as the bedrock of the NKPA's military policy, or *kunsa chŏngch'aek,* and advocates the following four objectives: (1) the militarization of the populace, (2) a stronghold-based fortified country, (3) a cadre-based army, and (4) the modernization of its military equipment.

Point 1 of the Four-Point Military Guideline is the militarization of the populace, or *chŏninmin ŭi mujanghwa.* Beginning its major efforts in the early 1960s, North Korea has now succeeded in arming much of its population. Civilians between the ages of fourteen and sixty, or more than 30 percent of the entire population, are subject to being mobilized to serve in North Korean's military forces. Currently, reserve troops number some 7.7 million, and each reservist is subject to being called upon to perform fifteen to thirty days of annual training.

Reserve forces are categorized into four groups. The Reserve Military Training Unit (RMTU) is the NKPA's principal reserve combat

---

* Article 60, chapter 4 (Defense) of the Socialist Constitution, revised on 9 April 1992, justifies the Four-Point Military Guideline; the 1998 revised constitution also specifies the same guidelines "Article 60: Self-reliant national defense can only be achieved by first arming the military and the people with political ideology, and on this foundation, instilling cadre potential in every soldier, modernizing the entire military, arming the entire population and turning the whole nation into a fortress."

force. Totaling approximately 620,000 personnel—men between the ages of seventeen and forty-five and single women between the ages of seventeen and thirty—serve in one of thirty-seven RMTU divisions.

The Worker and Peasant Red Guard resembles a civil defense force and numbers some 5.72 million personnel, mostly men between forty-six and sixty years of age. The primary mission of this force is to provide homeland defense, farming, and industry support. Its secondary mission is to provide troop replacements for both conventional and unconventional forces.

The third type of reserve is the Red Youth Guard, which is a military organization of middle school and high school students (ages fourteen to sixteen), and its membership totals some 940,000 youth. The fourth and smallest reserve force is the paramilitary troops, which numbers some 420,000 personnel and includes the Ministry of People's Security, Logistics Mobilization General Bureau, and Speed Battle Youth Shock Brigades.[5]

Point 2 of the military guideline calls for a stronghold-based fortified country, or *chŏn'gukt'o ŭi yosaehwa*. As mentioned earlier, North Korea has built an elaborate array of underground facilities throughout the country, particularly near the demilitarized zone. These facilities not only allow for the staging of units and equipment to facilitate a preemptive attack, but they also provide protection for troops and equipment during artillery and air attacks. Since being alerted to possible amphibious operations on its coasts, North Korea has also erected an elaborate coastal defensive system.

Point 3 of the guideline is a cadre-based army, or *chŏn'gun ŭi kanbuhwa*. The NKPA, with its active duty force strength of about 1.2 million personnel (organized in 19 corps-level units, including 9 infantry corps, 4 mechanized corps, 1 armored corps, 1 artillery corps, P'yŏngyang Defense Command, Border Guard Command, Missile Guidance Bureau, and Light Infantry Instruction Guidance Bureau),* developed a cadre-based military policy for rapidly expanding its combat strength during

---

* Major combat units comprise more than 170 divisions and brigades, including 80 infantry divisions and brigades, 30 artillery brigades, 10 armor brigades and 7 armor regiments, 20 mechanized brigades, and 25 special warfare brigades.

wartime mobilization. The principle of this guideline is the development of a professional cohort of leaders who are well trained in government ideology and modern military tactics and are thus prepared to assume higher levels of responsibility. For example, the four forward infantry corps are each designated for elevation as field army headquarters during wartime.

The fourth point of the guideline focuses on the modernization of its military equipment, or *kunchangbi ŭi hyŏndaehwa*. Despite suffering economical hardships over the past decade, North Korea's pursuit of equipment modernization over the past forty years has remained steady. In 2004 North Korea announced an annual defense budget of 15.5 percent of the government budget, or about 30 percent of its gross national product. Because of fiscal constraints, North Korea seeks to increase its military capabilities through minimal fund expenditures. This is best illustrated in its development and procurement of asymmetric weapons systems—including missiles, chemical, and biological munitions—and its continued development of nuclear weapons.

With its robust arsenal of ballistic missiles, of which more than half are chemical and nuclear weapons-capable, the NKPA can range all of South Korea with its SCUD-B/C short-range surface-to-surface guided ballistic missiles,* and all of Japan with its *Nodong* and *Taepodong*-1 medium-range ballistic missiles (both tested in the 1990s). The army could also reach Alaska and Hawaii with its 2-stage *Taepodong*-2 intercontinental ballistic missiles (ICBM), and anywhere in the United States with its 3-stage *Taepodong*-2 ICBM, both of which could be operational within the next decade.[6]

North Korea has an assessed stockpile of between 2,500 and 5,000 tons of chemical agents that includes blood, blister, choking, and nerve agents. The country also has an active biological weapons research program, with a probable inventory that includes anthrax, botulism, cholera, hemorrhagic fever, plague, smallpox, typhoid fever, and yellow fever.[7]

---

* SCUD-B is a transporter-erector-launcher (TEL) that can fire a single 1,000 kg high explosive or chemical warhead at a range of about 300 km. SCUD-C is an enhanced-range version of the SCUD-B.

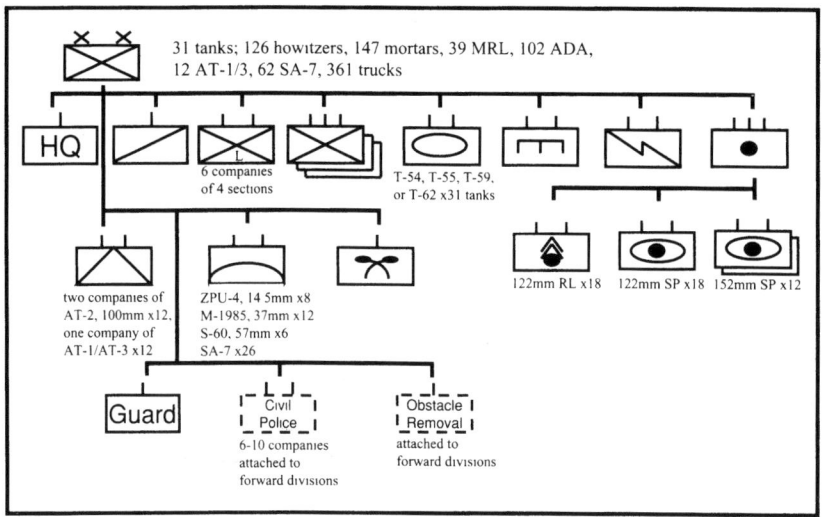

FIGURE 10. NKPA Infantry Division Organization Chart, 2000
KEY: XX = division; III = regiment; II = battalion; I = company; AT = antitank;
HQ = headquarters; L = light infantry; SP = self-propelled; double slash = infantry;
single slash = reconnaissance; arc = air defense; lazy E = engineer; lightning bolt =
signal; circle = artillery; oval = armor; dashed box = attached unit.
Source: Chŏk ŭl alcha (I): yŏndaegŭp isang pukkoegun chŏnsulgyori (Seoul: Korean
Army Headquarters, 2000), 214.

On 10 February 2005, P'yŏngyang declared that it possessed nuclear weapons; and while unproven experts surmise that currently the DPRK could possess as many as six to eight plutonium warheads.[8]

North Korean military experts believe that these missile, chemical, biological, and nuclear weapons programs measurably contribute to the country's security from external threats and that they complement its conventional military capabilities.

The main heavy weaponry of the NKPA's ground forces consists primarily of Soviet- and Chinese-made tanks, mechanized vehicles, field artillery pieces, and air-defense artillery systems. In addition to the tank units of the NKPA's armored and mechanized corps, the four front-line infantry corps each have 325 tanks, which are assigned to the corps's armor brigade and to each division's thirty-one-tank armored battalion.[9]

The NKPA has an aggregate of 3,700 tanks, including the older Soviet-model T-54 and T-55, the Chinese model T-59, and the more recent domestically manufactured T-62 Chŏnmaho tank. The NKPA's armored vehicle fleet totals 2,100 vehicles and consists chiefly of the wheeled BTR series, type M-1973, and a lesser quantity of the track-mounted BMP-series armored vehicles. Including multiple rocket launchers (MRL), the NKPA has approximately 13,500 field artillery pieces, ranging in caliber from 107-mm to 240-mm for its rocket artillery, and 100-mm to 170-mm for its cannon artillery. The NKPA also possesses a large array of air-defense artillery systems, totaling about 15,600 pieces. Representative of these weapons are the SA-7 and SA-16 shoulder-fired models and a variety of wheeled and tracked mounted gun and missile models, including the SA-2, SA-3, and SA-5-type systems (see figure 10 for standard NKPA infantry division).[10]

MILITARY STRATEGY/군사전략/軍事戰略

In accordance with its military strategy,* or *kunsa chŏllyak,* and for the purpose of fighting a quick, decisive war, the NKPA task organizes its units with a mix of regular combat forces, called *taebudae,* and special operations force teams, called *sobudae.* The combined employment of these two forces is referred to as mixed tactics. In short, based on the firm foundation of a three-pronged military strategy—surprise attack; quick, decisive war; and mixed tactics—North Korea believes it can launch an attack on South Korea that will successfully overwhelm the ROKA throughout the depths of the battlefield, thus causing the defeat of its opponent and the seizure of the Korean peninsula before the United States and/or United Nations could adequately counter.

The concept of the NKPA's surprise attack strategy, or *kisŭb chŏllyak,* is that by attacking the enemy at an unexpected time and place and by employing unexpected means, it can maximize time, speed, and secrecy. This strategy, coupled with an effective deception plan, is believed to yield maximum effects with minimum effort.

North Korea plans extensive and varied asymmetrical large-scale operations throughout the depths of the peninsula. According to the

---

* Military strategy is the highest component of military art; and concerns both the theory and practice of preparing a nation and armed forces for war. In the applied sense, military strategy determines the strategic mission of the armed forces and the forces necessary to achieve these missions.

strategies described above, the NKPA plans to initiate combat by conducting massive conventional and chemical cannon and missile bombardments while simultaneously employing SOF teams, numbering more than one hundred thousand personnel, to conduct sequential operations in the ROKA rear area.

The NKPA is organized around its light infantry, trusting that it can exploit the advantages of a light force, which facilitates stealthy nighttime mobility and unrestricted mountainous terrain maneuverability. The army sees this strategy as an opportunity to gain and maintain the initiative, thereby dictating to its opponent when and where to fight and thus gaining a tactical and psychological advantage.

Although the NKPA strategies may appear to be reasonably sound, North Korea lacks the economical resources to successfully fight and win a protracted war. Therefore, its strategy of quick, decisive war, or *sokchŏn sokkyŏl chŏllyak,* is to defeat South Korea before the United States military can intervene. After launching a massive asymmetrical first strike, North Korea intends to lead the attack with its forward infantry corps/armies by exploiting the initiative and to maintain the momentum by surging deep into ROKA territory with its armored and mechanized corps.

Originally trained and armed by the former Soviet Red Army, the NKPA continues to use as its underlying doctrine the Soviet military model, which was adapted to conform to the Korean terrain and the NKPA's light infantry-based military structure. The NKPA's SOF guerilla tactics are a derivation of Mao Zedong's military principles, as learned during the anti-Japanese guerrilla war, Chinese civil war, and the Korean War. Current NKPA tactics dictate using a mixture of mutually supporting conventional forces and SOF teams. Specifically, conventional forces depend upon SOF teams for intelligence collection and to facilitate setting the conditions for future operations, while SOF teams rely heavily upon conventional forces for logistic support.

PRINCIPAL FUNDAMENTALS OF WAR/원 준칙/原 準則

Combined-arms operation is the essential element of operational and tactical battle in NKPA doctrine, which is based on its five fundamental principles of war, or *wŏn chunch'ik:* mass and dispersion, surprise attack, increased maneuverability, cunning and personified tactics, and secure secrets.* These principles of war serve as a type of lens that is used at all levels of command to plan and execute offensive and defensive military operations.

Mass and Dispersion/집중과 분산/集中分散

Adherence to the principle of mass and dispersion, or *chibchung punsan,* is simply the process of managing the finite resource of combat power, which ensures the proper distribution of such resources between the main and supporting efforts. Mass and dispersion involves: (1) concentrating combat power at the decisive time and place; (2) weighting the main effort by attacking with at least twice the defender's combat power; (3) assigning the main effort a narrow front and dispersing the supporting effort over a wide front in order to hold and deceive the enemy, while reducing losses from high-casualty-producing weapons; (4) maximizing terrain and considering the deception operation when dispersing; and (5) avoiding excessive concentration and indiscriminate dispersion.

Surprise Attack/기습/奇襲

The NKPA employs the tactics of surprise attack, or *kisŭb,* by attacking with a bold and courageous force at an unexpected place and time and with unexpected means. A surprise attack involves: (1) utilizing inclement weather, hours of darkness, and rugged terrain; (2) developing clever deception plans and employing skilled infiltration teams; (3) conducting parachute and air assault operations; (4) setting mass fires; (5) quickly concentrating the effects of combat power at a decisive area; and (6) employing large-scale mechanized units.

Increased Maneuverability/기동성 증대/機動性 增大

The core strategy of the NKPA is to fight and win a quick, decisive war. To facilitate this objective, combat units attempt to use terrain to their advantage, while employing the NKPA principles of increased

---

* Prinicples of war are the basic guidelines for organizing and conducting battles, operations, and war as a whole. These principles are idealistic; they show what an army would like to do, but not, in all cases, what it might be capable of doing.

maneuverability, or *kidongsŏng chŭngdae:* (1) employing both ground and air transportation assets to quickly maneuver infantry, artillery, and armor formations on the battlefield; (2) utilizing existing high-speed road networks; (3) conducting night moves and utilizing minor roads and steep terrain to stealthily maneuver; (4) hastening mobility by conducting raids and employing SOF teams; and (5) emphasizing maneuverability as a basic element of combat power.

Cunning and Personified Tactics/기묘하고 영활한 전술/奇妙靈活戰術

Because of the NKPA's advantage over the ROK military in terms of troop numbers, and its perceived superior political ideology, the NKPA believes that it can develop and execute superior operations, utilizing its cunning and personified tactics, or *kimyo hago yŏnghwalhan chŏnsul.* For the NKPA, cunning is used in planning and executing all military operations; therefore, as appropriate, these cunning attributes should always be applied: (1) consideration of tactical cunning when employing combat troops; (2) exploitation of the initiative by leaders; (3) proactive aggressiveness; (4) bold and perceptive leadership; (5) no hesitation; (6) closely held, perfect comprehensive plans; and (7) fast estimates and bold operations that facilitate a quick, decisive war.

Like Sun Tzu, the NKPA believes that because all warfare is based on deception, every operations plan should therefore include a deception story. Four typical cunning maneuvers are: "East Sound West Attack," or *tongsŏngsŏkyŏk*/동성서격/東聲西擊 (Demonstration); "East Strike West Attack," or *tongkyŏksŏsŭb*/동격서습/東擊西襲 (Feint); "Hit and Run," or *ilhaengch'ŏlli*/일행천리/一行千里 (Raid); and "Instigate Fratricide," or *mangwŏnchŏnsul*/망원전술/望遠戰術.

Secure Secrets/비밀보장/秘密保障

The fifth principle of war is to secure secrets, or *pimil pojang.* To accomplish this principle, the NKPA maintains a close hold on classified materials while actively circulating false materials. Some of the methods used include employing reconnaissance activities and security counter-measures, applying complete camouflage, propogating clever deceptions and stratagem, exploiting counterintelligence activities, and conducting operations in darkness and inclement weather.

Principles of war are an enduring foundation of military doctrine, which is built on a sound basis of warfighting theory and practical experience. Through a serious application of its five principles of war—mass and dispersion, surprise attack, increased maneuverability, cunning and personified tactics, and secure secrets—the NKPA believes that it will be victorious on the battlefield.

ORDER OF THE FATHERLAND LIBERATION WAR VICTORY 40TH ANNIVERSARY COMMEMORATION (Chokuk Haepang Chŏnjaeng Sŭngni 40tols Kinyŏm Hungjang)

Established 10 March 1993

In commemoration of the Liberation War, this award was presented to the servicemen and laborers who had contributed to the victory of the Liberation War. The award is fashioned as a 60-mm-diameter ten-point shield of long silver rays that are joined in the center by a 33-mm-diameter gold ring with a red background. In the center of the ring is a soldier who is holding aloft the DPRK flag. On the obverse is written *Chokuk Haebang Chŏnjaeng Sŭngni 40tols Kinyŏm Hungjang* (Order of the Fatherland Liberation War Victory 40th Anniversary Commemoration), with a pin back. (Art by Matthew S. Minnich)

· 6 ·

Offensive Tactics/공격전술/攻擊戰術

OFFENSE, THE DECISIVE form of war, is executed by NKPA operational and tactical forces to achieve two stated purposes: the annihilation of enemy forces, and the seizure of key terrain. While conducting simultaneous and sequential attacks, and encirclement operations, the NKPA seeks to deny opposing forces the ability to reorganize or reconstitute.[1] To support the operational commander's offensive operation, SOF teams are simultaneously infiltrated throughout the enemy's rear area to conduct strikes against critical targets and to create general confusion and fear.

According to the situation and its opponent's actions, the NKPA plans three types of offensive operations—attack against a defending enemy, attack against an attacking enemy, and attack against a retreating enemy—defined in terms of the posture of the belligerents.

An attack against a defending enemy is the first basic form of NKPA offensive operations, and is defined in relation to the degree and strength of the defending forces. The enemy situation dictates the forms of maneuver employed and the time available for planning and preparation.

The second basic form of NKPA offensive operations is an attack against an attacking enemy. This operation is a clash between opposing sides when both are striving to fulfill their assigned missions, and include, an attack against a counterattacking force, a counterstriking force, or in a meeting engagement while attempting to occupy key terrain. The goal of such combat is to rapidly rout the enemy, seize the initiative, and to create advantageous conditions for subsequent operations.

Attack against a retreating enemy is the third basic form of NKPA offensive operations. Its goal is to exploit the success of an attack by destroying a fleeing force.

The NKPA uses two forms of troop movement before initiating an attack: approach march and attack formation. The NKPA uses an approach march when direct contact with an enemy is intended. This movement is employed when the attacking force is certain of the enemy's location. As the enemy is assaulted by a barrage of concentrated indirect fires, the attacking force deploys into battle formation about 1 km from the enemy's forward positions.

The NKPA uses the attack formation when contact with the enemy is imminent. Regiments depart their assembly position in battalion formation; then about 3 km to 5 km from the enemy's defensive position, battalion formations split into company formations. Between 2 km and 3 km of the enemy's defensive position, company formations split into platoon formations. Lastly, within 1 km of the enemy's forward defensive line, platoon formations deploy into combat formations in preparation to launch their attack.

Based on terrain, combat force ratios, obstacles, and the commander's concept of operations, NKPA forces employ seven forms of maneuver: penetration, thrust, holding, turning, infiltration, besetment, and encirclement (see figure 11, which depicts the seven forms of maneuver on an NKPA situation map). While typically employed in combinations, each form of maneuver attacks the enemy differently.

PENETRATION MANEUVER/돌파/突破

An NKPA penetration maneuver, or *tolp'a*, is unlike a U.S. Army doctrinal penetration, which is employed to destroy a defending unit. Rather, an NKPA penetration is executed by the first tactical echelon (1TE) for the singular purpose of creating a maneuver corridor that is sufficiently wide enough to allow passage of the follow-on second tactical echelon

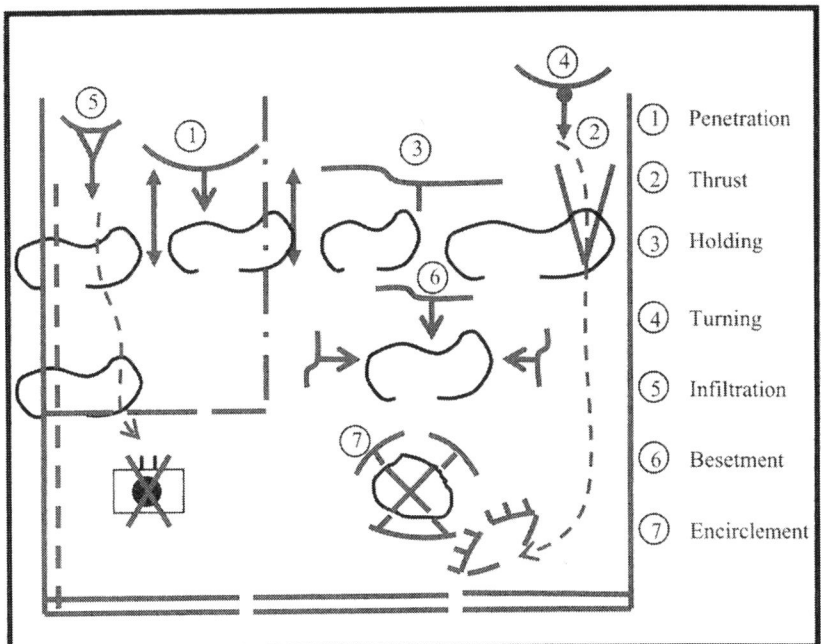

Figure 11. NKPA Forms of Maneuver
NKPA Maneuver Graphics Legend: solid vertical and dashed lines = corps boundary; single solid vertical line = divisional boundary; dashed and dotted vertical line = regimental boundary; single dashed horizontal line = 1TE regiment's limit of advance (LOA); double dashed horizontal line = 2TE LOA; double two-headed arrows = zone of action of main effort; dashed arrow = direction of movement for infiltration unit and/or turning unit; hashed oval = turning unit's location for establishing an encirclement; incomplete oval-type shape = opponent's battle position; crossed-out unit symbol = infiltration unit's target; numbers 1–7 graphically depict the seven forms of maneuver.
Source: *Chŏk ŭl alcha (I): yŏndaegŭp isang pukkoegun chŏnsulgyori* (Seoul: Korean Army Headquarters, 2000), 51.

(2TE) (see table 1). The 1TE penetrates the front-line defense and establishes a hasty defensive position along a forward slope. The 2TE follows by maneuvering unhindered from the line of departure to the NKPA's 1TE's limit of advance, where it continues to press the fight deep into its opponent's rear area (see table 2).

Penetration maneuvers are division-level operations. In setting the conditions for a penetration, between fifty and eighty tubes of artillery, mortar, and rocket fire are allocated to penetrate each kilometer of a standard defensive position. The indirect-fire ratio is nearly tripled, to include an allocation of 150 to 180 tubes per kilometer when attacking

Table 1. NKPA Standard Attack Dimensions

Unit Area	Army	Corps	Div	Regt	Bn
Front (km)	40–60	20–40	10–16	3–6	1.5–2
Depth (km)	80–100	40–50	10–15	5–7	2–3

Source: *Chŏk ŭl alcha (I): yŏndaegŭp isang pukkoegun chŏnsulgyori* (Seoul: Korean Army Headquarters, 2000), 45–207.

through the current general observation post (GOP) line, located along the Korean demilitarized zone.

THRUST MANEUVER/첨입/尖入

A thrust maneuver, or *ch'ŏmip*, is planned for piercing a strong point. This concept can be compared to using a wedge for splitting wood. Like a wedge, the NKPA uses a small ground force to pierce a portion of an enemy's defense; once pierced, follow-on forces exploit the situation for the purpose of executing one of four missions: (1) continuing the attack by striking the flank, or rear area of the pierced unit; (2) attacking the flank, or rear area of an adjacent unit; (3) assisting the passage of either a turning maneuver force or a besetment maneuver force (see below); or (4) opening a blocked maneuver corridor. When using the thrust to create a large maneuverable gap, thrust units may be employed in pairs, with one unit operating on each side of the gap (see figure 12).

Thrust maneuvers are typically conducted by a company, battalion, or regiment and are executed by three attack formations. For example, during a battalion-level operation, three companies in tandem assault an area approximately six hundred to eight hundred meters so as to

Table 2. NKPA Second Tactical Echelon
Standard Penetration Width

Follow on force (2TE)	Corps	Div	Regt
Penetration Width	8–12 km	4–6 km	2–3 km

Source: *Chŏk ŭl alcha (I): yŏndaegŭp isang pukkoegun chŏnsulgyori* (Seoul: Korean Army Headquarters, 2000), 45–207.

Thrust Maneuver in order to attack a flank and/or rear.	Thrust Maneuver in order to clear a blocked route.

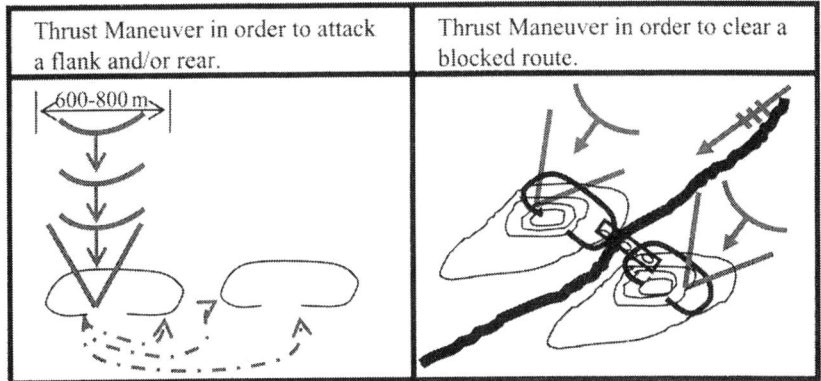

FIGURE 12. Thrust Maneuver
Source: *Chŏk ŭl alcha (I): yŏndaegŭp isang pukkoegun chŏnsulgyori* (Seoul: Korean Army Headquarters, 2000), 58.

puncture a gap in the defensive position. To set the condition for a thrust maneuver, between 110 and 150 tubes of artillery, mortar, and rocket fire are allocated when attacking a strong point; between 150 and 180 tubes are allocated when attacking through the current GOP line along the demilitarized zone. The maximum attacking frontage for a thrust maneuver is one kilometer.

HOLDING MANEUVER/견제/牽制

A holding maneuver, or *kyŏnje*, is a form of attack that employs the principle of dispersion. The intent of this maneuver is to fix a larger force with a much smaller one, thereby inducing the committal of the enemy reserve force into that area, away from the main effort. This operation is conducted when a supporting effort feints or demonstrates across a broad front while the main effort penetrates or thrusts along a narrow front.* As the main effort attacks to the limit of its advance and the 2TE follows by attacking deep into the opponent's rear area, attempting to induce a retreat of the forward defending element. When the defending force begins to disengage, the NKPA holding maneuver unit begins a forward

* A feint is a form of attack used to deceive the enemy as to the location or time of the actual decisive operation. Forces conducting a feint seek direct fire contact with the enemy but avoid decisive engagement. A demonstration is a form of attack designed to deceive the enemy as to the location or time of the decisive operation by a display force. Forces conducting a demonstration do not seek contact with the enemy.

TABLE 3. NKPA Standard Defense Frontage

Echelon	Div	Regt	Bn	Co
Frontage	16–20 km	8–10 km	3–4 km	1–1.5 km

Source: *Chŏk ŭl alcha (I): yŏndaegŭp isang pukkoegun chŏnsulgyori* (Seoul: Korean Army Headquarters, 2000), 45–207.

attack, pushing the opposing force into an encirclement position, where it will attempt to destroy that force.

The holding maneuver is typically performed from company to division level. Executing units are employed along a standard defense frontage and avoid decisive combat by creating a credible deception through the effective employment of small-unit raids and the massing of indirect fires (see table 3).

TURNING MANEUVER/우회/迂廻

Unlike the U.S. Army's doctrinal turning movement, which is used to maneuver in the enemy's rear to force it to abandon its defensive position and to attack in an undesirable direction, the NKPA turning maneuver, or *uhoe*, has a different objective. The purpose of an NKPA turning maneuver is to either establish an encirclement position in the enemy's rear area or to conduct a besetment of an enemy defensive position. Taking advantage of poor nighttime visibility, inclement weather (rain or snow), and rough terrain (swamps, rice paddies, reservoirs, or large rivers), this movement is conducted by maneuvering undetected through the gaps of defending units. In the absence of a natural gap, the turning maneuver force exploits the gap that is created by either a penetrating or thrusting force.

Corps- and army-level headquarters conduct operational turning maneuvers, while division and lower headquarters conduct tactical turning maneuvers (see table 4).

INFILTRATION MANEUVER/침투/浸透

An infiltration maneuver, or *ch'imt'u*, is a covert movement of NKPA forces through opposing lines (within range of sight and sound) to

TABLE 4. Turning Maneuver: Unit Employment Size and Mission

Echelon	Size	Mission	Employment area
Corps	Regt × 1	Establish blocking position	Vicinity of planned
Div	Bn × 1	to the rear of the	encirclement position
Regt	Co × 1	encirclement position;	and area intended to
Bn	Plt × 1	and block reinforcements	block reinforcements

Source: *Chŏk ŭl alcha (I): yŏndaegŭp isang pukkoegun chŏnsulgyori* (Seoul: Korean Army Headquarters, 2000), 45–207.

establish attack positions in the opponent's rear area. During an infantry corps-level offensive operation, two-thirds of the strength of both the corps's light infantry brigade and sniper brigade (four battalions each) are employed to conduct raids upon command and control centers and artillery positions, and to secure choke points along the axis of advance. During an infantry division-level offensive operation, the division's light infantry battalion employs four of its six light infantry companies as infiltration units.

Light infantry units—specifically designated for infiltration maneuvers—are not organic or assigned to infantry regiments or battalions;* therefore, at these lower levels of command, regular infantry units conduct infiltration maneuvers against critical targets within the command's area of operation (AO). Infantry regiments typically employ one infantry company, and battalions employ one infantry platoon to conduct infiltration maneuvers in their respective AOs. Whether in the offense or defense, infiltration maneuvers are always used to support NKPA combat operations (see table 5).

BESETMENT MANEUVER/포초/包秒

Regiment and lower echelons conduct a besetment maneuver, or *p'och'o*, which like a U.S. Army encirclement maneuver is designed to destroy opposing forces in strong points. Doctrinally, the attacking force is three times greater than the defending force; hence, regiments attack battalion strong points, and battalions attack company strong points. In an effort to inflict maximum casualties, direct-pressure forces maintain contact

* An organic element is one that is assigned to and forms an essential part of a military organization. An assigned element is one that is placed in an organization on a relatively permanent basis.

TABLE 5. Infiltration Maneuver Unit Employment Size and Mission

Echelon	Employment area	Size	Missions*
Corps	Lt Inf Bn × 4; and Sniper Bn × 4	Corps AO	1. Destroy C2 nod
Div	Lt Inf Co × 4; and	Div AO	2. Destroy wpn position
Regt	Inf Co × 1	Regt AO	3. Secure chokepoint
Bn	Inf Plt × 1	Bn AO	

Source: *Chŏk ŭl alcha (I): yŏndaegŭp isang pukkoegun chŏnsulgyori* (Seoul: Korean Army Headquarters, 2000), 45–207.
*Mission type can be the same irrespective of echelon.

with the defender on multiple flanks to prevent its disengagement and reconstitution.

The NKPA executes four types of besetments, which are classified as attacks from (1) the front and one flank; (2) the front and two flanks; (3) the front and rear; or (4) the front, two flanks, and rear. Regardless of the besetment type employed, the NKPA always engages with indirect fires the enemy's flanks that are not assaulted by maneuver and direct fire.

ENCIRCLEMENT MANEUVER/포위/包圍

Offensive operations are routinely planned with the intent of conducting an encirclement maneuver, or *p'owi*. An encirclement maneuver is planned in the enemy's rear area where the majority of a retreating force can be intercepted, encircled, and destroyed. Such locations are always positioned between the reserve force and the front-line defense. It is expected that once a penetration or thrust maneuver is successfully executed, adjacent defending units will withdraw to rearward or alternate positions. The NKPA believes that opposing forces are the most vulnerable during a withdrawal, and are therefore more easily destroyed with encirclement maneuvers.

Corps- and army-level headquarters employ up to two divisions when conducting operational encirclements; and tactical encirclements, which are conducted by division and lower headquarters, typically employ their entire unit to execute this operation. There are four types of

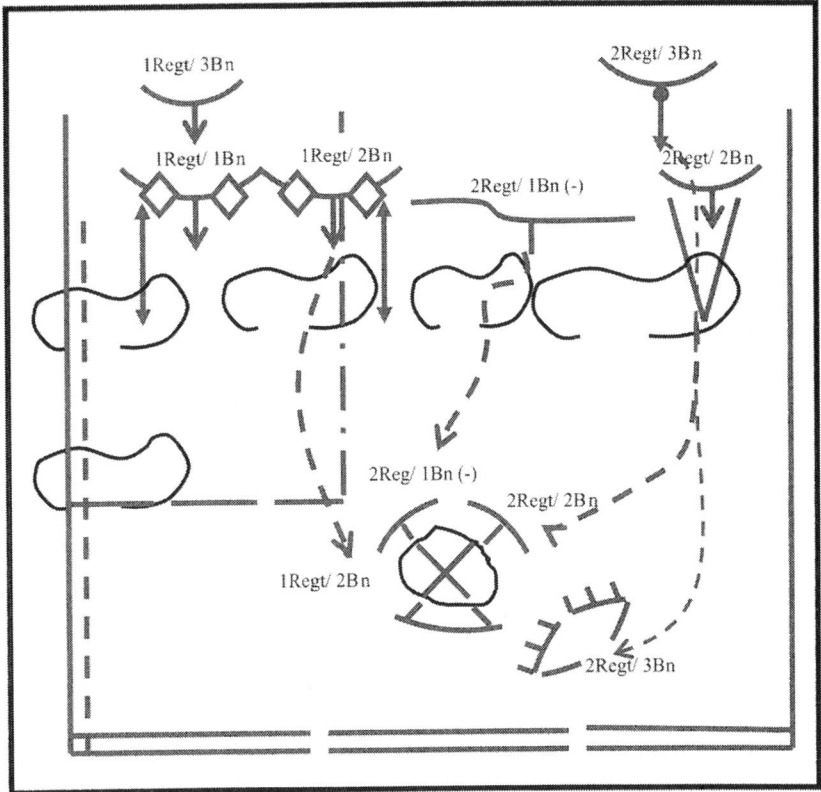

FIGURE 13. Division Encirclement Maneuver—Unit Employment
NKPA Maneuver Graphic Legend: combination solid and dashed vertical lines = corps boundary; single vertical line = division boundary; dashed and dotted vertical line = regiment boundary; single dashed horizontal line = 1TE regiment's limit of advance (LOA); double dashed horizontal line = 2TE LOA; double two-headed arrows = location of penetration; dashed arrow = direction of movement for encirclement maneuver units; hashed oval = location where the turning movement unit will establish the rear limit of the encirclement; incomplete ovals = opponent's battle positions; inverted arc with arrow = infantry unit; diamonds = attachment of tanks; wavy horizontal line with stubby perpendicular line = holding unit; inverted arc with circle and arrow = turning movement unit; V = location of thrust; crossed circle – encirclement location.
Source: *Chŏk ŭl alcha (I): yŏndaegŭp isang pukkoegun chŏnsulgyori* (Seoul: Korean Army Headquarters, 2000), 70–71.

encirclement maneuvers: a partitioned destruction, for the encirclement of a large force; a compressed destruction, for the encirclement of a small force; a fire-power destruction, for the destruction of forces in narrow areas and while fighting encirclement operations; and a raid destruction, for the annihilation of forces in built-up areas (see figure 13).

ORDER OF THE DPRK FOUNDATION 20ᵀᴴ ANNIVERSARY COMMEMORATION (Chosŏn Minjujuŭi Inmin'gonghwakuk Ch'anggŭn 20 Chunyŏn Kinyŏm Hunjang)

Establish 24 May 1968

Awarded for contributing to the development of the nation while working in a government office, work organization, national economic organ, or social association. This award is fashioned as a 55-mm-diameter disc that is decorated with a golden laurel wreath. On top of the wreath is a five-point golden star that is 60-mm in diameter. Inside the star is a 2.5-mm-wide golden ring that is 32-mm in diameter. In the ring is a golden national emblem that is 27-mm high and 22.5-mm wide, which is fastened to a white plate. A waving national flag is on the top of the golden star. On the obverse are the words *Chosŏn Minjujuŭi Inmin'gonghwakuk Ch'anggŭn 20 Chunyŏn Kinyŏm Hunjang*, the issue number, 1968.9.9, with a pin back.

Source: *Nodong Sinmun* (P'yŏngyang) 25 May 1968. (Art by Matthew S. Minnich)

• 7 •

Defensive Tactics/방어전술/防禦戰術

THE NKPA EMPLOYS two types of defensive tactics, or *pangŏ chŏnsul*—
mobile defense and area defense—as a temporary interval between attacks, thereby allowing it to gain time and conserve troop strength.[1]
NKPA defensive operations are specifically planned for one of four purposes: to repulse a superior strengthened attacking force; to inflict grave
casualties upon an attacking force; to defend key terrain; or to transition
to a decisive attack.

MOBILE DEFENSE/기동방어/機動防禦

A withdrawing unit employs the mobile defense, or *kidong pangŏ,* as it
trades space for time. The primary characteristic of a mobile defense is
that the main combat power is concentrated in the second echelon while
the first echelon fights a scries of delaying actions that disrupt its enemy
until it is engaged in the decisive fight.

AREA DEFENSE/진지방어/陣地防禦

The area defense, or *chinji pangŏ,* is the NKPA's principal defensive
tactic and is used to hold key terrain or to destroy an attacking force.

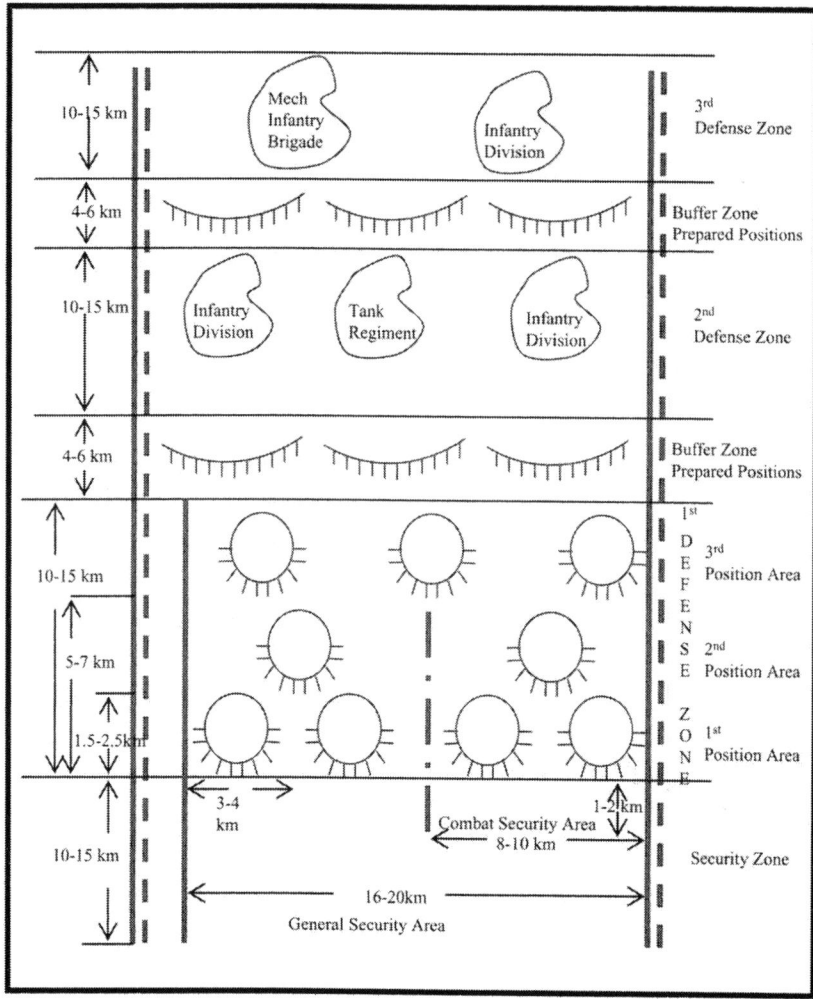

FIGURE 14. NKPA Field Army Area Defense Zone Formation
Source: *Chŏk ŭl alcha (I): yŏndaegŭp isang pukkoegun chŏnsulgyori* (Seoul: Korean Army Headquarters, 2000), 155.

The integration of indirect and direct fires and the use of obstacles, cover, concealment, and deception are integral to the area defense. The sine qua non of this basic defense structure, however, is the antitank defense system, which incorporates a layered series of antitank (AT) positions and a planned location from which to counterattack the enemy's main attacking units (see below).

The first echelon, in an area defense, is composed of two-thirds of the defending force, while the remaining one-third of the force is arrayed in the second echelon. Additionally, one-ninth of the total combat force, which is tasked from the second echelon, makes up the reserve. Another one-ninth of the total combat force, which is tasked from the first echelon, is used as the regimental and battalion security element.

A field army area defense zone is organized into four zones: farthest forward is the security zone, followed thereafter by the first, second, and third defensive zones (see figure 14).

SECURITY ZONE

The security zone is divided into two sectors—combat security area and general security area—and has a frontage equal to that of the first echelon's defensive zone (division area is sixteen to twenty kilometers) and a depth of ten to fifteen kilometers (see table 6).

Combat Security Area

The combat security area extends one to two kilometers in front of the first defensive zone and is subdivided into two areas. The first area

TABLE 6. Security Area

Security area	Security element	Purpose	Loc fwd of defense	Unit size
General Security Area	General Security Outpost (GSOP)	Atk Warning Delay Interdiction	10–15 km	Corps: Regt + Div: Bn +
Combat Security Area	Combat Outpost (COP)	Atk Warning Raid Prevention Indirect-fires Observation	1–2 km	Regt: Co + Bn: Plt +
	Direct Security	Atk Warning Raid Prevention	200–400 meters	Sentry; Security Patrols; Ambush Patrols

Source: *Chŏk ŭl alcha (I): yŏndaegŭp isang pukkoegun chŏnsulgyori* (Seoul: Korean Army Headquarters, 2000), 45–207.

TABLE 7. NKPA Standard Defensive Area

Echelon	Div	Regt	Bn	Co
Frontage	10–16 km	8–10 km	3–4 Km	1–1.5 km
Depth	10–15 km	5–7 km	1.5–2.5 km	1 km

Source: *Chŏk ŭl alcha (I): yŏndaegŭp isang pukkoegun chŏnsulgyori* (Seoul: Korean Army Headquarters, 2000), 45–207.

extends between two hundred and four hundred meters in front of the forward battalions and is occupied by security outposts, security patrols, and ambush teams. The second area extends up to two kilometers in front of each forward regiment and is occupied by a company plus–sized element, which is arrayed in three to four combat observation posts. The mission of these combat observation posts is to provide early attack warning, prevent surprise attacks, and to call for and adjust mortar and artillery fires.

General Security Area

The general security area is employed during corps and division operations and is positioned in front of the combat security area, which extends ten to fifteen kilometers in front of the first echelon defensive zone.* During corps operations an enhanced regiment occupies the general security area, and during division operations an enhanced battalion occupies this area. The mission of the general security outpost (GSOP) is to provide attack warning and to conduct delay and interdiction operations.

FIRST DEFENSIVE ZONE

The 1TE division—or main defensive echelon—occupies the first defensive zone. This zone has a standard frontage of sixteen to twenty kilometers and a depth of ten to fifteen kilometers (see table 7). This zone is further divided into three defensive areas. The four forward battalions of the two forward regiments occupy position area one, while the two rear battalions of the forward regiments occupy position area

---

* While the general security area is a doctrinal templated zone, it is not likely to be employed, due to the anticipated proximity of opposing forces.

two. The division's 2TE regiment is arrayed in three battalions abreast and occupies position area three.

SECOND AND THIRD DEFENSIVE ZONES
AND BUFFER ZONES

During army and corps operations, divisions occupy the second and third defensive zones. The missions of these units are to reinforce the first defensive zone and to conduct infiltration and counterattack operations. A four- to six-kilometer buffer zone typically separates the defensive zones. These buffer areas include prepared positions which are intended for future occupation by the second and third defensive zone forces to either halt penetration of the first defensive zone or to prepare for transition to the attack.

ANTITANK DEFENSE SYSTEM

Area defense operations are designed to support the antiarmor battle. In other words, defensive positions are selected based on the enemy's predicted attack route and in what location along that route the NKPA plans to fight the antiarmor battle. Such battles are divided into six phases and encompass both the indirect- and direct-fire fights. The six phases are the antiarmor obstacle plan; the antiarmor fire plan; the antitank defensive position; the antitank engagement area; the employment of the counterattack force; and the employment of the antitank reserve (see figure 15).

Antiarmor Obstacle Plan

Obstacles are emplaced in front of the forward defensive positions of the combat security area and within each antitank engagement area. The obstacle belts are tied into the terrain and have a mix of antipersonnel (AP) and antitank (AT) mines, which are used to separate ground forces from mechanized forces. Each obstacle belt is well camouflaged, observed, and covered by fire. The obstacle belts are multitiered and positioned at the maximum range of the various antitank weapon systems, ranging from about four hundred to one thousand meters.

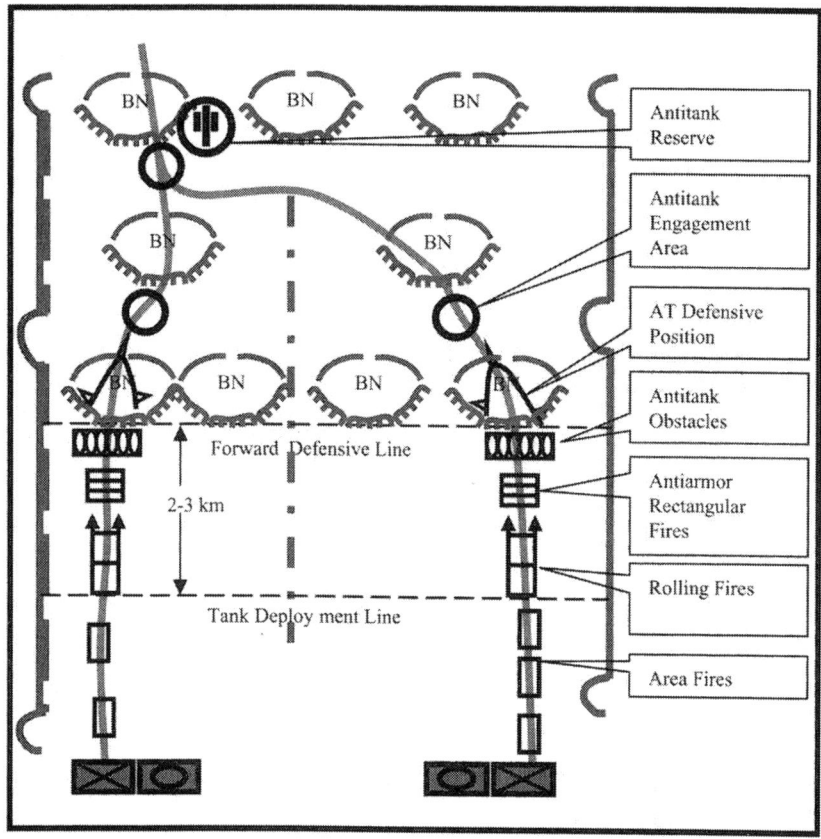

FIGURE 15. Antitank Defense System
Source: *Chŏk ŭl alcha (I): yŏndaegŭp isang pukkoegun chŏnsulgyori* (Seoul: Korean Army Headquarters, 2000), 190.

ANTIARMOR FIRE PLAN

The antiarmor fire plan is divided into four phases—area fires, rolling fires, antiarmor rectangular target fires, and direct fires. The first three phases are fired with indirect-weapon systems, and the fourth phase is fired with direct-fire weapons (see table 8).

Phase One: Area Fires

In phase one, area fires are planned at choke points along the route of advance, which are located approximately two to eight kilometers in

Table 8. Indirect Phase Fires

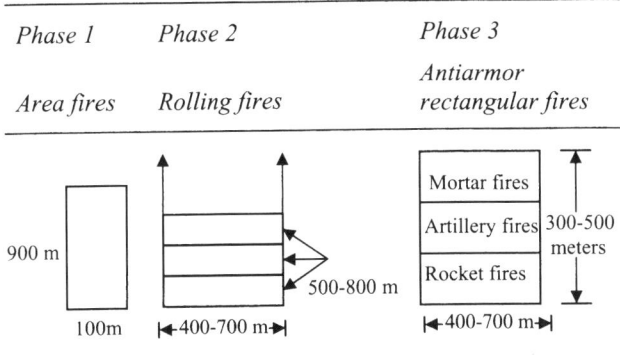

Phase 1	Phase 2	Phase 3
		Antiarmor
Area fires	*Rolling fires*	*rectangular fires*

Source: *Chŏk ŭl alcha (I): yŏndaegŭp isang pukkoegun chŏnsulgyori* (Seoul: Korean Army Headquarters, 2000), 45–207.

front of the defensive position. Sequentially, these targets are engaged by rockets, artillery, and mortars. The requisite number of firing units are preplanned according to the anticipated number of attacking tank companies. As an initial planning figure, two artillery battalions are allocated to engage each enemy tank company. According to target saturation requirements, either a battery or a battalion engages a standard rectangular target of about one hundred meters by nine hundred meters in size.

Phase Two: Rolling Fires

In phase two, rolling fires are planned two thousand meters in front of the defensive position. These fires are employed to disrupt and destroy armor units that are transitioning from the march to a battle formation. These fires are between four hundred and seven hundred meters in breadth and are fired about every five hundred to eight hundred meters, for a maximum of four firing iterations.

Phase Three: Antiarmor Rectangular Target Fires

In phase three, antiarmor rectangular targets are fired immediately following phase two fires. While these fires are similar in purpose to phase two fires, density and timing are its distinguishing features. The target width—about four hundred to seven hundred meters—is the same as in phase two fires; however, it has a target depth of about three hundred to five hundred meters, and the attack is made in three sequential volleys of indirect fire. Typically, one to three targets are fired from the conclusion of phase two fires until the opposing force reaches the obstacle belt.

Phase Four: Direct Fires

In phase four, direct fires begin at the forward defensive-line obstacle belt, where tanks, antitank guns (100-mm SU-100 guns and 76.2-mm SU-76 guns), recoilless rifles (82-mm B-10 guns), and man-packed 40-mm RPG-7 grenade launchers begin firing at maximum ranges while NKPA infantry soldiers engage the advancing ground forces. Final protective indirect fires are planned within three hundred meters of NKPA ground forces and are undertaken to disrupt and destroy units attempting to breach the defensive position.

ANTITANK DEFENSIVE POSITION

The main effort battalion's antitank defensive position is planned by the regimental commander and is typically situated on a parallel forward ridgeline so that maneuvering tanks can be attacked in crossfire. Typically, antitank defensive positions are organized by task, with one recoilless rifle platoon (three guns) attached to the main effort company; one platoon of SU-76 antitank guns (two guns); and several RPG-7 grenade launchers, employed in teams of two and three weapons (see figure 16).* As advancing armor formations enter the position, antitank obstacles halt the column, allowing antitank weapons to first engage the front and rear vehicles followed by a mass engagement of all other vehicles in the column.

ANTITANK ENGAGEMENT AREA

The second stage of the antitank direct-fire fight occurs in the antitank engagement area. This engagement area is established at both regimental

---

* An attached element is one that is placed in an organization temporarily.

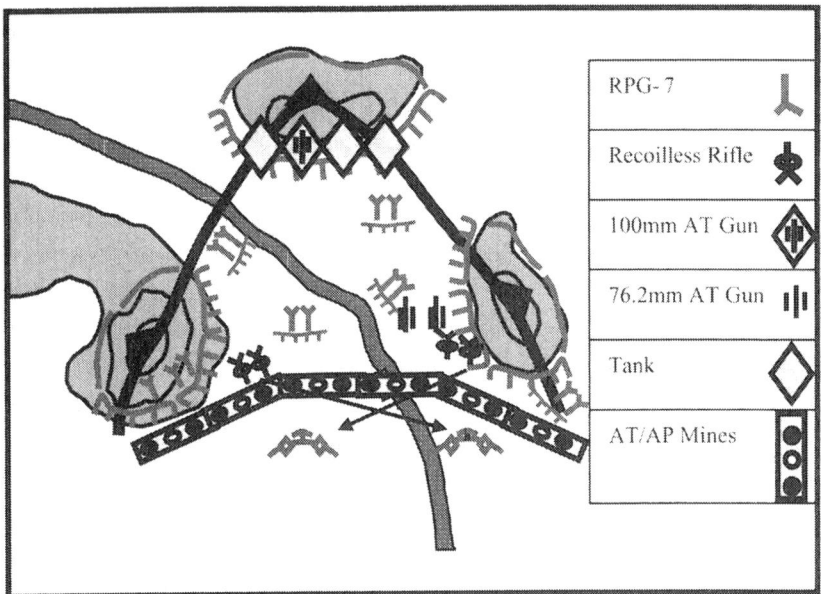

RPG-7	
Recoilless Rifle	
100mm AT Gun	
76.2mm AT Gun	
Tank	
AT/AP Mines	

FIGURE 16. Antitank Defensive Position
Source: *Chŏk ŭl alcha (I): yŏndaegŭp isang pukkoegun chŏnsulgyori* (Seoul: Korean Army Headquarters, 2000), 195.

and divisional levels. Advancing formations that are not destroyed by the forward defensive positions are reengaged in decisive combat in the antitank engagement area. As with defensive positions, engagement areas are established in depth (1TE and 2TE). Antitank engagement areas are typically task-organized, with two SU-100 howitzer platoons and one or two RPG-7 platoons. However, based on allocation it is also possible for antitank engagement areas to be augmented by a limited number of tanks and recoilless rifles (see figure 17).

ANTITANK MOBILE RESERVE

The antitank reserve is a mobile reserve designed to destroy tanks that successfully bypass antitank defensive positions and antitank engagement areas. Division units are task-organized with two reserve antitank companies positioned on the battlefield between the 1TE and 2TE.

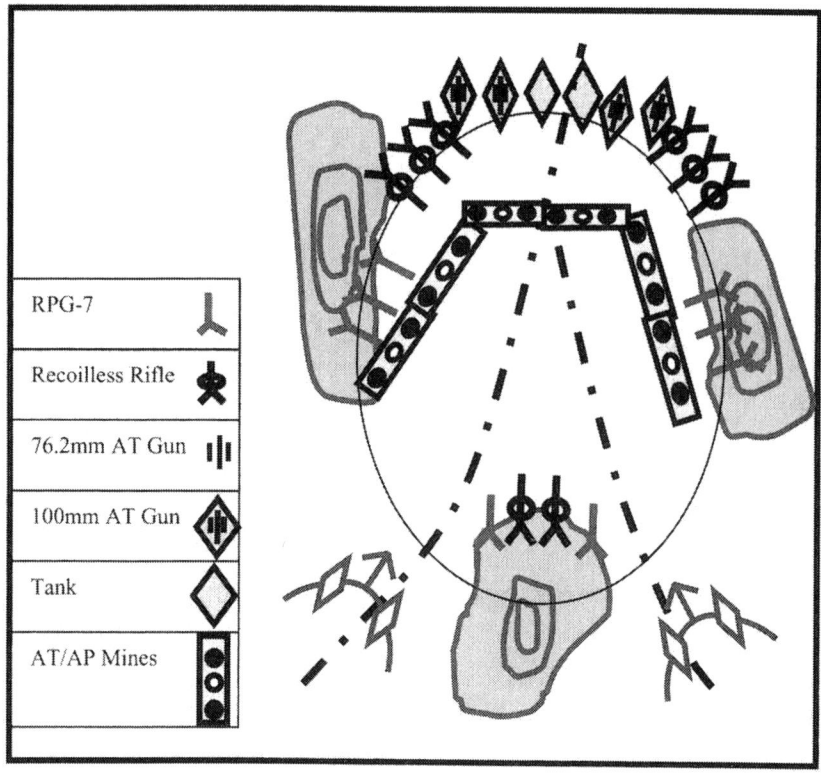

RPG-7	
Recoilless Rifle	
76.2mm AT Gun	
100mm AT Gun	
Tank	
AT/AP Mines	

FIGURE 17. Antitank Engagement Area
Source: *Chŏk ŭl alcha (I): yŏndaegŭp isang pukkoegun chŏnsulgyori* (Seoul: Korean Army Headquarters, 2000), 197.

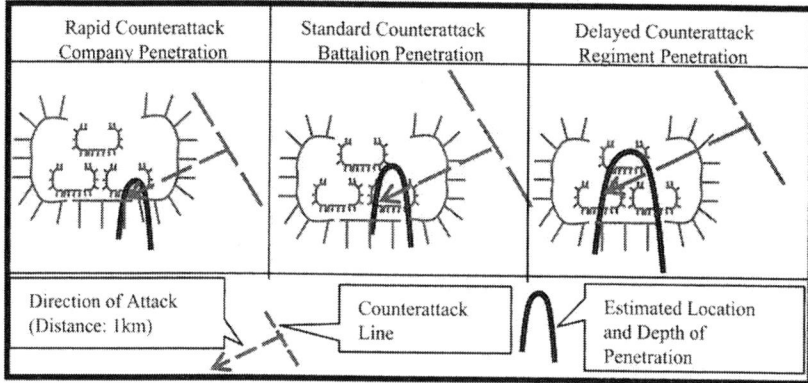

FIGURE 18. Division Level Counterattack Employment Options
Source: *Chŏk ŭl alcha (I): yŏndaegŭp isang pukkoegun chŏnsulgyori* (Seoul: Korean Army Headquarters, 2000), 200.

TABLE 9. Counterattack Type/Criterion

Unit / Type	Regiment	Division -Std Operation-	Corps
Raid Counterattack	Penetration of 1TE Plt	Penetration of 1TE Co	Penetration of 1TE Bn
Standard Counterattack	Penetration of 1TE Co	Penetration of 1TE Bn	Penetration of 1TE Regt
Delayed Counterattack	Penetration of 1TE Bn	Penetration of 1TE Regt	Penetration of first defensive zone

Source: *Chŏk ŭl alcha (I): yŏndaegŭp isang pukkoegun chŏnsulgyori* (Seoul: Korean Army Headquarters, 2000), 45–207.

COUNTERATTACK FORCE

Headquarters at the regimental level and above plan counterattack operations to halt and destroy opposing forces that penetrate the defense position. Such operations are intended to set the condition for transitioning to the attack. During the planning phase of the operation, the counterattack position is selected based upon the predicted point of penetration. The counterattack position is usually situated on a forward ridgeline approximately one kilometer to the rear flank of the penetrated unit. Based on such factors as which terrain will best support a counterattack and the criticality of the defensive positions, commanders select either a rapid, standard, or delayed counterattack location (see figure 18 and table 9). Typically, a second echelon force headquarters conducts the counterattack. For example, during a division defensive operation, where the first and second regiments are deployed in the main defensive area, the third regiment would be used as the counterattacking force.

ORDER OF THE THREE GREAT REVOLUTIONS RED FLAG
(3-Tae Hyŏngmyŏng Puk ŭn Ki Hunjang)
Established 20 November 1986

Worn on the left breast next to the Second-class National Flag Order, this award is presented to three revolution red-flag pacesetters for supporting the leadership of the NKWP, and pushes forward the course of the revolutions under the slogans of ideology, technology, and culture in accordance with the *chuch'e* idea. The award is fashioned as a 60-mm-diameter ten-point shield of long silver rays. At the center of the shield is a 33-mm-diameter gold laurel wreath with a portion of a mechanical gear at the top and a mounted flying Pegasus in the center. On the top of the ten-point shield is a red flag and 3-*Tae Hyŏngmyŏng Puk ŭn Ki Hunjang* written in gold. On the obverse is written 3-*Tae Hyŏngmyŏng Puk ŭn Ki Hunjang* (Order of the Three Great Revolutions Red Flag), with a pin back.

Source: *Nodong Sinmun* (P'yŏngyang) 22 November 1986. (Art by Matthew S. Minnich).

• 8 •

Artillery Grouping Tactics/포병전술/砲兵戰術

INTEGRATED FIRE SUPPORT is a decisive element on the battlefield. In the offense, it is the key means in achieving an advantageous correlation of forces over an opponent. It can create gaps in defenses; immobilize, disrupt, or destroy enemy combat formations; and repel counterattacks. In the defense, it disrupts enemy attack preparations, causes attrition among advancing forces, and repels forces that have reached or penetrated the defense perimeter.

Artillery support assets include organizations, weapons, target acquisition means, and munitions. Artillery or fires units of the NKPA are equipped with rockets, howitzers, mortars, and recoilless guns; organized by weapon type; and assigned to a headquarters to perform a specified mission (see table 10).[1] The NKPA's artillery formations are assigned to four levels of command—battalion, regiment, division, and corps.

The organic artillery or fires assets of a battalion are generally limited to a single mortar company of nine 82-mm mortars and one recoilless rifle platoon of three 82-mm B-10 guns.

A regiment is organized with a mortar battalion of eighteen 120-mm mortars; an antitank company of six 76.2-mm SU-76 self-propelled

TABLE 10. Unit Organic Artillery Weapon Systems

Sec	Mortar	Recoil. Gun	AT Gun	Arty	Rocket	ADA
Bn Arty	**Co** × **1** 82 mm × 9	**Plt** × **1** 82 mm × 3				
Regt Arty	**Bn** × **1** 120 mm × 18		**Co** × **1** 76.2 mm × 6	**Bn** × **1** 122 mm × 18	**Btry** × **1** 107 mm/ 140 mm × 9	**Bn** × **1** 14.5 mm × 20
Div Arty			**Co** × **2** 100 mm × 12 **Co** × **1** AT-1/3 × 12	**Bn** × **2** 152 mm × 24 **Bn** × **1** 122 mm × 18	**Bn** × **1** 122 mm × 12	**Bn** × **1** 14.5 mm × 8 37 mm × 12 57 mm × 6
Corps Arty				**Bn** × **6** 170 mm × 108	**Bn** × **6** 240 mm × 108	**Regt** × **1** 14.5 mm × 8 57 mm × 36

Source: *Chŏk ŭl alcha (I): yŏndaegŭp isang pukkoegun chŏnsulgyori* (Seoul: Korean Army Headquarters, 2000), 45–207.

(SP) guns; an artillery battalion of eighteen 122-mm howitzers; one multiple rocket launcher (MRL) battery of either nine 107-mm M-1992 rocket launchers or 140-mm RPU-14 rocket launchers; and one air defense artillery (ADA) battery of twenty 14.5-mm ZPU-4 towed guns.

A division has a three-company antitank battalion, of which two companies each have six 100-mm SU-100 SP guns, and one company has either twelve 140-mm AT-1 missiles or twelve 120-mm AT-3 missiles. A division also has three artillery battalions, of which two of the battalions have twelve 152-mm howitzers, and one battalion has eighteen 122-mm howitzers; one MRL battalion of twelve 122-mm M-1992 rocket launchers; and an ADA battalion of eight 14.5-mm ZPU-4 towed guns, twelve 37-mm M-1985 SP guns, and six 57-mm S-60 towed guns.

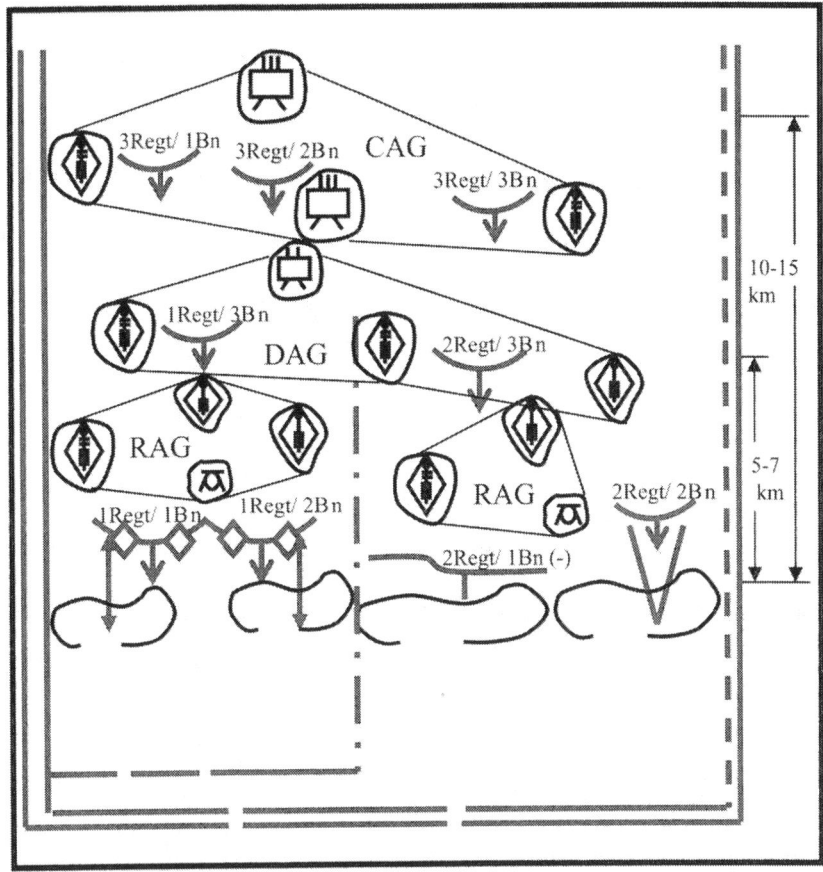

Figure 19. Standard NKPA Artillery Positioning Tactics (Attack)
NKPA Maneuver Graphic Legend: vertical solid and dashed lines = corps boundary; single vertical solid line = division boundary; dashed and dotted vertical lines = regiment boundary; single dashed horizontal line = 1TE regiment's limit of advance (LOA); two dashed horizontal lines = 2TE LOA; two double-headed arrows = penetration location; dashed arrow = encirclement maneuver units' direction of movement; hashed oval = encirclement location rear limit, established by turning movement unit; incomplete ovals = opponent's battle positions; inverted arc with arrow = infantry unit; diamond = tank attachment; wavy horizontal line = holding unit; inverted arc with circle and arrow = turning movement unit; V = thrust location; crossed circle = encirclement location.
Source: *Chŏk ŭl alcha (I): yŏndaegŭp isang pukkoegun chŏnsulgyori* (Seoul: Korean Army Headquarters, 2000), 203.

A corps has twelve artillery battalions—six cannon battalions and six rocket battalions. Each cannon battalion has eighteen 170-mm M-1989 SP howitzers, and each rocket battalion has eighteen 240-mm M-1991 truck-mounted MRLs. The corps also has an organic ADA

TABLE 11. Indirect Fire Systems Graphics

Mortar	Rocket	Heavy SP Howitzer High Angle	Med SP Howitzer High Angle	SP Howitzer Low Angle
60mm	107mm	152mm and 170mm	122mm	0-100mm
82mm	122mm-200mm			101mm-150mm
120mm	240mm			151mm; higher
160mm				

Source: *Chŏk ŭl alcha (I): yŏndaegŭp isang pukkoegun chŏnsulgyori* (Seoul: Korean Army Headquarters, 2000), 45–207.

regiment, which is equipped with eight 14.5-mm ZPU-4 towed guns and thirty-six 57-mm S-60 towed guns.

The basic mission of all North Korean artillery units is to defeat and destroy personnel, equipment, and facilities, and to support maneuver—both infantry and armor-operations. Artillery units are task-organized into artillery groups at the regiment, division, and corps levels.

REGIMENTAL ARTILLERY GROUPS

The regimental artillery group (RAG) provides fire support to its infantry regiment and is generally organized with between two and four organic or attached mortar and artillery battalions. Generally, the mortar battalion is positioned on the rear slope of a hill located up to one and one-half kilometers to the rear of the front line. The 122-mm and 152-mm artillery battalions are deployed forward of the regiment's second echelon battalions.

DIVISION ARTILLERY GROUP

The division artillery group (DAG) is typically organized with three to five organic and/or attached artillery and rocket battalions. The DAG is positioned forward of the division's 2TE regiments.

CORPS ARTILLERY GROUP

The corps artillery group (CAG) is generally organized with three to six organic and/or attached artillery and rocket battalions. The CAG is positioned behind the lead division's 2TE. When a corps fights with three divisions abreast, three CAGs of four battalions each typically support the corps. However, when the corps is arrayed with two divisions abreast, it typically forms two CAGs of six battalions each (see figure 19 and table 11).

Appendixes

• A •

A Historic Review

Protruding from the eastern border of Manchuria, the Korean peninsula divides the Yellow Sea (West Sea) from the Sea of Japan (East Sea) and lies geographically encircled by the great powers of China, Japan, and Russia.

China has been Korea's northern neighbor since time immemorial, although its border has not always been contiguous. In a like manner, despite the fact that China ruled as suzerain until the late nineteenth century, its relationship with Korea has not always been amicable.[1] During the four-hundred-year period from 108 BC to AD 313, Han commanderies occupied military outposts throughout Korea, exacting tribute as they deemed appropriate. Following the expulsion of the last Han commandery, in the fourth century, Korea managed to maintain its national identity throughout the succeeding sixteen centuries, lasting until the end of Korea's Chosŏn Dynasty in 1910. Throughout the majority of this period, Korea used diplomacy to maintain its independence. However, on many occasions, peace was preserved only through force of arms, including defending against China's Sui Dynasty in 598 and its T'ang Dynasty in the 660s; the Khitan invasions between 993 and 1018; and the Jurchên (or proto-Manchu) invasions from 1107.[2] The most destructive incursion from the north was inflicted by the Mongols in 1231 and persisted until the fall of its Yüan Empire in 1368.[3] In the waning days of the Yüan Dynasty, a powerful brigand force called the Red Turbans crossed the frozen Amnok River with forty thousand men and conquered Sŏkyŏng (modern-day P'yŏngyang). A year later, in 1361, the Red Turbans attacked again, with a force of about one hundred thousand troops, and advanced south until the force eventually culminated at Kaesŏng, the Koryŏ (ancient Korea) capital. Although the Red Turbans were eventually routed, Koryŏ's combat power was stretched dangerously thin.

Korea's southeastern neighbor is Japan. Although ancient relationships between the two nations were generally aloof, since at least the thirteenth century there have been several eras of great hostility. From the early thirteenth century through the sixteenth century, Japanese pirates known as *Wakō* regularly raided Korea's coastal towns.[4] Korea's Koryŏ dynastic government countered this threat by deploying military forces from its northern border to areas along its southern coastline. However, by the late sixteenth century, what had otherwise been a tolerable relationship between Korea and Japan turn acrid as Japanese regent Toyotomi Hideyoshi invaded Korea in 1592 and 1598 in a thwarted attempt to conquer China and Korea. The destructive magnitude of the Imjin War ingrained in the Koreans a deep disdain for the Japanese. The death of Hideyoshi in 1598 quickly facilitated the accession of his lieutenant, Ieyasu Tokugawa, in 1603 and the state's self-induced sequestering until the rise of Japan's Meiji emperor in the mid-nineteenth century.

The West's opening of Japan in 1857 revealed a side of Japan that most of her people were unaccustomed to—her "primitive backwardness." Emerging from two and one-half centuries of self-induced seclusion, Japan's lack of exposure to the modern world had inhibited its ability to accurately assess its own comparative development. As a result of this revelation, Japan quickly undertook a whole-scale approach of adopting Western techniques and developments. The breadth and rapidity of the mimicry that followed conveys a sense of the disquietude and desperation with which Japan transformed. In much the same way that Japan adopted Western cultural and institutional structures, it also appropriated its imperialist practices. The reasons for imperialism are as varied as they were for Japan when the country opted to follow that route in the closing decades of the nineteenth century; such pretenses surely included the loss of national prestige, perceptions of looming Western encroachment into East Asia, and the thought of economic advancement.

As Japan was "opened" in the later half of the nineteenth century, the internationally astute Western nations impressed "unequal treaties" upon Japan, resulting in a perceived loss of national prestige, or *kokui*. Left humiliated and smarting after an international slighting, Japan thereafter became easily agitated by other international confrontations, particularly those among its neighbors. As a result, Japan's early foreign policies were shaped by a near obsessive concern with enhancing its national prestige.

By 1890, although no longer concerned about Western encroachment upon its own territories, Japanese leaders feared that Western nations might attempt to colonize the country's weaker neighbors, which might then threaten Japan's own interests. Obsessed with the prospect of being encircled by Western imperial powers, Japan embarked upon a policy of preemption; in other words, in order to protect its own interests, Japan sought to colonize its weaker neighbors before the West was able to do so.

Meiji leaders, like the leaders of Western imperialist states, saw an inextricable linkage between economic competition and political competition, between economic penetration and territorial expansion. During Japan's conversion from an agrarian nation to an industrial nation, many people left the field for the factories. Hence, the Japanese needed a supplemental source of agricultural products to sustain its people; penetrating Korea would not only fill that void, but it would also provide a market for some of Japan's manufactured products. In the words of historian Peter Duus, "it thus becomes difficult to disentangle the economic motives behind Japan's expansion [into Korea] from its search for international prestige and its strategic anxieties."[5]

In 1860 Czarist Russia expanded its territorial control deep into Siberia, extending southeast to the Ussuri River, where it established a naval port at Vladivostok. Since then, Russia has shared a short contiguous border along Korea's northeastern coastline. A quarter of a century after creating the Vladivostok naval port, the Russian government sought to extend its reach south into Korea, where it could open a warm-water naval port. To this end, Russia signed a treaty with Korea in 1884, but was thwarted in its port efforts by the combined powers of Britain, China, and Japan.[6]

By the late nineteenth century, the expansionist policies of Japan and Russia collided in Korea, where China already exercised suzerainty. As China was more firmly entrenched in Korea than was Russia, Japan first sought to dislodge China from the peninsula, resulting in the Sino-Japanese War of 1894–1895. Having been militarily defeated, China relinquished suzerainty over Korea by signing the Shimonoseko Treaty.[7] Initially being awarded the Manchurian Liaodong peninsula as an indemnity from the war, a Russian-led international effort quickly prevented Japan from laying claim to the area.

While stymieing Japan's expansion into Manchuria, Russia concurrently diminished Japan's burgeoning political influence in Korea by sheltering Korea's King Kojong in the Russian legation in Seoul from February 1896 to February 1897. As a result, pro-Russian politicians emerged, replacing politicians who had previously favored aligning Korea closer to Japan. In 1898 Russia negotiated a secret deal with the Chinese, authorizing a twenty-five-year lease of two naval ports at Dalian and Lüshun (Port Arthur), the latter being located on the earlier-contested peninsula of Liaodong. With the establishment of naval ports at Vladivostok, Russia, and Liaodong, China, it became clear that Russia would have to control Korea if it hoped to effectively command and control the naval fleets stationed at these distant ports. As neither Russia nor Japan was willing to relinquish its ambition of controlling Korea, rising tensions led to the Russo-Japanese War of 1904–1905.

Russia's defeat on the battlefield left Japan's ambitions unchecked in East Asia, thus facilitating its planned seizure of Korea. Moving quickly after the Russo-Japanese War, Itō Hirobumi, the first resident-general (tōkan) of Korea, secured the Korean government's reluctant consent to the installment of Japan's protectorate government, or residency-general (tōkanfu) as it was termed in 1905. Over the next five years, Japan embedded itself in all aspects of the Korean government while it systematically extricated Koreans from the same governing process. Finally, Korea's six-thousand-man army was disbanded on 1 August

1907, which left Korea helpless in preventing Japan from annexing it, just three years later, on 22 August 1910.[8]

Hundreds of disbanded Korean soldiers joined one of the many anti-Japanese guerrilla bands called Righteous Armies, or *ŭibyŏng*. For some five years the *ŭibyŏng* fought against the Japanese invaders, but by the end of 1910, major organized resistance within Korea had been effectively quelled as some 17,600 *ŭibyŏng* fighters lay dead.[9] Those who continued to resist the Japanese with armed force sought refuge in Manchuria, and for the next two decades, light resistance emanated from north of the Amnok and Tumen Rivers. The Japanese invasion of Manchuria in 1931, however, stroked the flame of resistance, uniting Chinese and Korean partisans in a renewed fight against their Japanese overlords.

• B •

The Ten-Point Program of the Fatherland Restoration Association

1. A broad united anti-Japanese front shall be formed with the participation of the whole Korean nation to overthrow the rule of the piratical Japanese imperialists and establish a genuine people's government of the Korean people today.
2. In close alliance, the Korean and Chinese nations shall overthrow Japan and its puppet "Manchaca"; then the Chinese people shall establish a revolutionary government through elections, and the Korean residents in Chinese territory shall enjoy genuine autonomy.
3. The Japanese army, *gendarmerie,* and police as well as their lackeys shall be disarmed, and a revolutionary army, which will truly fight for the independence of Korea, shall be formed.
4. All the enterprises, railways, banks, ships, farms, and irrigation facilities owned by the Japanese government and Japanese individuals as well as the traitorous pro-Japanese elements' properties and land shall be confiscated to pay the expenses of the independence movement, and a portion of it shall be used for relieving the poor.
5. All bonds, taxes, and the monopoly systems of the Japanese and their lackeys shall be abolished; the life of the masses shall be improved; and the national industry, agriculture, and trade shall be duly developed.

6. Freedom of speech, the press, assembly, and association shall be achieved; the practice of Japanese terrorism and encouragement of feudalistic ideas be opposed; and all political offenders be released.

7. Difference between the nobility and commonalty and other inequalities shall be abolished; equality irrespective of sex, nationality, and religion be ensured; the social status of women be enhanced and their personality be respected.

8. Slave labor and enslavement education shall be abolished; forced military service and enforcement of military education for the youth be opposed; education carried on in our mother tongue; and compulsory free education be enforced.

9. An eight-hour day shall be put into effect; labor conditions be improved; wages raised; labor laws be enforced; the laws on various insurance for workers enacted by the state organ; and the unemployed working masses be relieved.

10. Those nations and states which approach the Korean nation on an equal basis shall be closely allied with; and comradely friendship shall be maintained with those states and nations which are sympathetically disposed while maintaining neutrality towards our national liberation movement.

Source: *Korean Revolutionary Museum* (P'yŏngyang: Foreign Languages Publishing House, 1963), 67.

• C •

North Korean Leadership, 1946-1948

NKIPC 9 Feb 1946 – 20 Feb 1947	NKPC 20 Feb 1947 – 9 Sep 1948	DPRK 9 September 1948
Chairman Kim Il Sung (K)	Chairman Kim Il Sung (K)	Premier Kim Il Sung (K)
Vice Chairman: Kim Tu-bong (Y) Chief Sec: Kang Yang-uk (N)	Vice Chairmen: Kim Ch'aek (K) Hong Ki-chu (N)	Vice Premiers: Kim Ch'aek (K) Hong Myŏng-hŭi (N) Pak Hŏn-yŏng (SK-N)
Bureau and Department Chiefs:	**Bureau and Department Chiefs:**	**Cabinet Ministers:**
Security: Ch'oe Yong-gŏn (K)	X	National Defense: Ch'oe Yong-gŏn (K)
X	People's Inspection: Ch'oe Ch'ang-ik (Y)	National Inspection: Kim Wŏn-bong (Y)
X	Foreign Affairs: Yi Kang-guk (SK)	Foreign Affairs: Pak Hŏn-yŏng (N-SK)
X	Internal Affairs: Pak Il-u (Y)	Internal Affairs: Pak Il-u (Y)
Agriculture and Forestry: Yi Sun-gŭn (N)	Agriculture and Forestry: Yi Sun-gŭn (N)	Agriculture and Forestry: Pak Mun-kyu (N-SK)
Commerce: Han Tong-ch'an (N)	Commerce: Chang Si-u (N)	Commerce: Chang Si-u (N)
Communications: Cho Yŏng-yŏl (N)	Communications: Chu Hwang-sŏp (N)	Communications: Kim Chŏng-ju (N)
Education: Chang Chong-sik (N)	Education: Han Sŏl-va (N)	Education: Paek Nam-un (N-SK)
Finance: Yi Pong-su (N)	Finance: Yi Pong-su (N)	Finance: Ch'oe Ch'ang-ik (Y)
Health: Yun Ki-yŏng (N)	Health: Yi Tong-yŏng (N)	Health: Yi Pyŏng-nam (N-SK)
Industry: Yi Mun-hwan (N)	Industry: Yi Mun-hwan (N)	Industry: Kim Ch'aek (K)
Justice: Ch'oe Yong-dal (N)	Justice: Ch'oe Yong-dal (N)	Justice: Yi Sŭng-yŏp (N-SK)
Labor Department: Unknown	Labor: O Ki-sŏp (N)	Labor: Hŏ Sŏng-t'aek (N-SK)
Transportation: Han Hŭi-chin (N)	Transportation: Ho Nam-hŭi (N)	Transportation: Chu Yŏng-ha (N)
General Affairs Department: Yi Chu-yŏn (N)	General Affairs Department: Kim Chŏng-chu (N)	City Management: Yi Yong (N)
Propaganda Department: O Ki-sŏp (N)	Propaganda Department Ho Chŏng-suk (Y)	Culture and Propaganda: Hŏ Chŏng-suk (*female*) (Y)
Planning Department: Chŏng Chin-t'ae (N)	Staff Department: Chang Chong-sik (N)	State Planning Commission: Chŏng Chun-t'aek (N)
X	Food Administrative Dept: Song Pong-uk (N)	Minister without Portfolio: Yi Kŭk-no (N)

Legend: (K) = *Kapanist*; (N) = native; (N = SK) = native from South Korea; (Y) = *Yananist*.

Source: Kim Ch'ang-sun, *Pukhan sibonyŏnsa*, 191, 192, 204, 205, 232, and 233.

• D •

North Korea's Military Command Structure, 2004

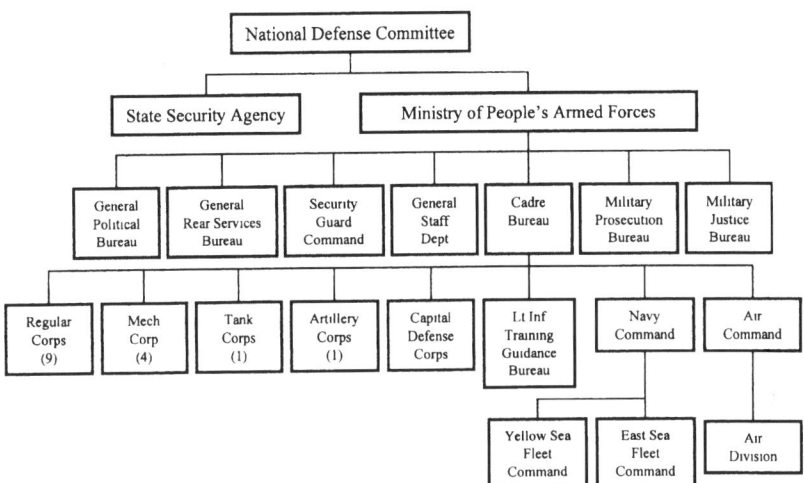

Source: Republic of Korea Ministry of National Defense. *Kukpang Paeksŏ: 2004* [Defense White Paper: 2004] (Seoul, Korea: Ministry of National Defense, 2004), 36.

• E •

NKPA Forward Infantry Corps, Organization Chart 2000

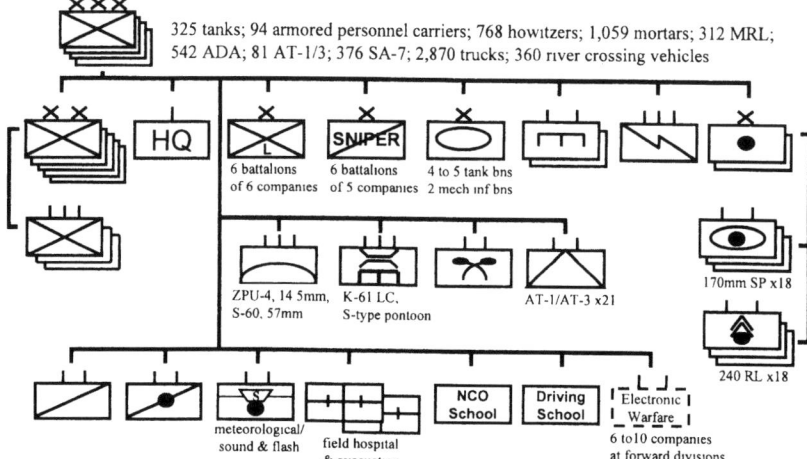

325 tanks; 94 armored personnel carriers; 768 howitzers; 1,059 mortars; 312 MRL; 542 ADA; 81 AT-1/3; 376 SA-7; 2,870 trucks; 360 river crossing vehicles

6 battalions of 6 companies

6 battalions of 5 companies

4 to 5 tank bns
2 mech inf bns

ZPU-4, 14 5mm, S-60, 57mm

K-61 LC, S-type pontoon

AT-1/AT-3 x21

170mm SP x18

240 RL x18

meteorological/ sound & flash

field hospital & evacuation

NCO School

Driving School

Electronic Warfare

6 to10 companies at forward divisions

KEY: XXX = corps; XX = division; III = regiment; II = battalion; I = company; AT = antitank; HQ = headquarters; L = light infantry; SP = self-propelled; double slash = infantry; single slash = reconnaissance; arc = air defense; lazy E = engineer; lightning bolt = signal; circle = artillery; oval = armor; dashed box = attached unit. Source: *Chŏk ŭl alcha (I): yŏndaegŭp isang pukkoegun chŏnsulgyori* (Seoul: Korean Army Headquarters, 2000), 215.

• F •

NKPA Infantry Regiment, 2000 (Organization Chart)

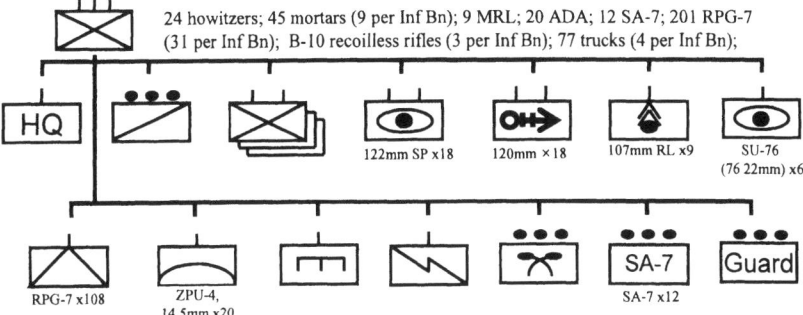

24 howitzers; 45 mortars (9 per Inf Bn); 9 MRL; 20 ADA; 12 SA-7; 201 RPG-7 (31 per Inf Bn); B-10 recoilless rifles (3 per Inf Bn); 77 trucks (4 per Inf Bn);

KEY: III = regiment; II = battalion; I = company; ••• = platoon; HQ = headquarters; L = light infantry; lazy E = engineer; SP = self-propelled; double slash = infantry; single slash = reconnaissance; arc = air defense; lightning bolt = signal; circle = artillery; oval = armor; inverted v = anti-tank; arrow = mortar; RL = rocket launcher
Source: *Chŏk ŭl alcha (I): yŏndaegŭp isang pukkoegun chŏnsulgyori* (Seoul: Korean Army Headquarters, 2000), 213.

• G •

Map of North Korea and Northeast China

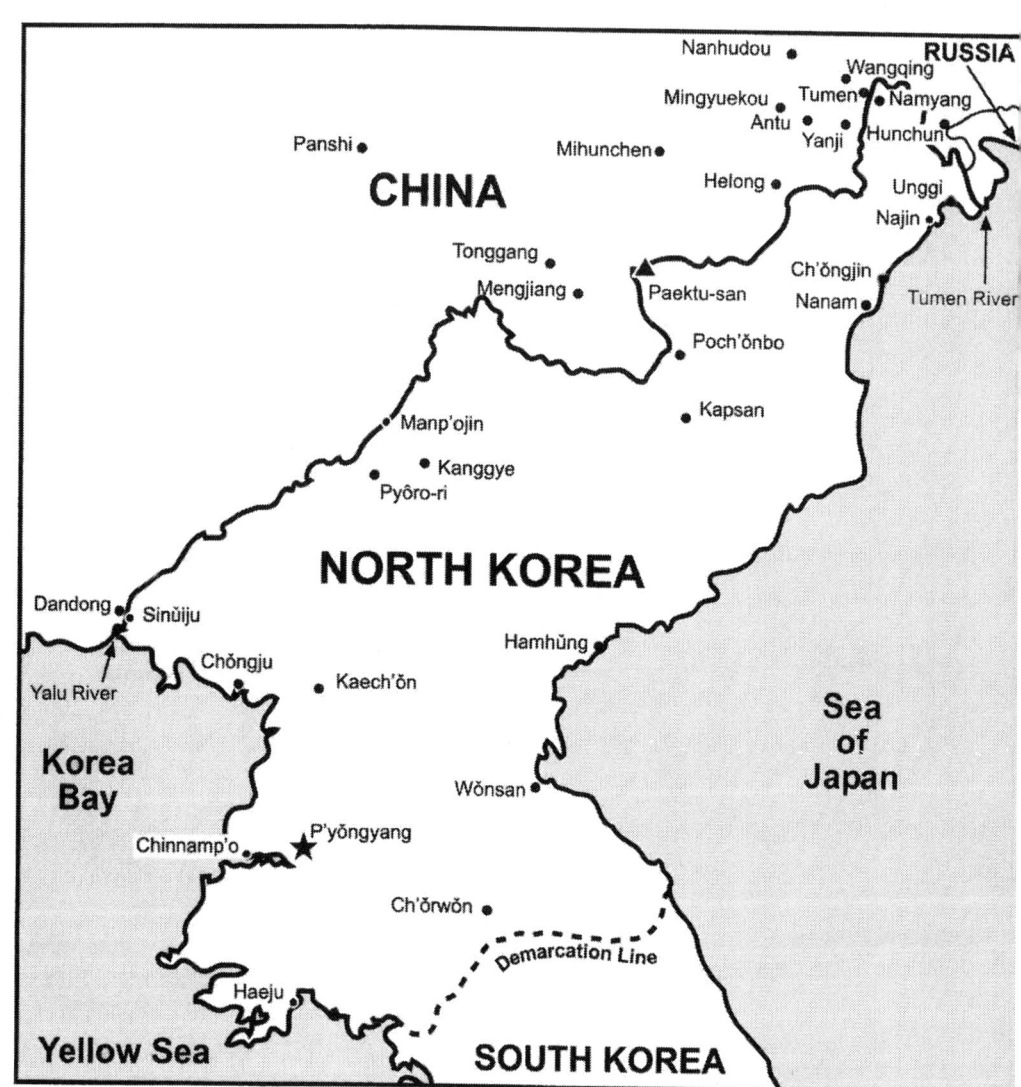

Art by Matthew S. Minnich

Notes

INTRODUCTION

1. Kim Il Sung, "Chosŏn Inmin'gun ch'anggun e chehayŏ: Chosŏn Inmin'gun yŏlbyŏngsik esŏ han yŏnsŏl, 8 February 1948" [On the occasion of the creation of the Korean People's Army: speech delivered at a review of the Korean People's Army, 8 February 1948], in *Kim Il Sung Sŏnjip* [Selected works of Kim Il Sung], vol. 2. (P'yŏngyang: Chosŏn Nodongdang Ch'ulp'ansa, 1964), 73–74.

2. Ibid., 78–79.

3. Kim Il Sung, "Chosŏn Inmin'gun ŭn hangil mujaeng t'ujaeng ŭi kyaesŭngja ida: Chosŏn Inmin'gun 324 kunbudae kwanha changbyŏngeŭl ap esŏ han yŏnsŏl, 8 February 1958" [The Korean People's Army is the successor to the anti-Japanese armed struggle: speech delivered before the officers and men of the 324th Army Unit of the Korean People's Army, 8 February 1958], in *Kim Il Sung Sŏnjip* [Selected Works of Kim Il Sung], vol. 5. (P'yŏngyang: Chosŏn Nodongdang Ch'ulp'ansa, 1960), 316–17.

4. *Nodong Sinmun* (Workers' Daily), (P'yŏngyang) 8 February 1978.

5. Ibid., 25 April 1978.

CHAPTER 1. EARLY ORIGINS OF THE (NORTH) KOREAN PEOPLE'S ARMY

1. Paek Pong, *Minjok ŭi t'aeyang Kim Il Sung Changgun* [General Kim Il Sung the sun of the nation], 1st ed., vol. 1 (P'yŏngyang: Inmun Kwahaksa, 1968), 94–95.

2. *Facts about Korea* (P'yŏngyang: Foreign Languages Publishing House, 1961, 25.

3. *Korean Revolutionary Museum* (P'yŏngyang: Foreign Languages Publishing House, 1963), 3. The full date of the organization of the Anti-Japanese Guerrilla Army was recorded in the March 1964 edition of the NKWP organ *Kŭlloja.* Kim Ŭl-jŏn, "Chosŏn Inmin Hyŏgmyŏnggun chojik 30 chunyŏn" [The 30th anniversary of the organization of the Korean People's Revolutionary Army], *Kŭlloja* [The Worker] 244 (March 1964): 31.

4. Paek, *Minjok ŭi t'aeyang*, 1st ed., vol. 1, 100.

5. Suh Dae-Sook, *Kim Il Sung: The North Korean Leader* (New York: Columbia University Press, 1988), 15–16.

6. Robert A. Scalapino and Chong-sik Lee, *Communism in Korea*, 2 vols. (Berkeley: University of California Press, 1972), part 2, 920.

7. Suh, *Kim Il Sung*, 31.

8. Paek, *Minjok ŭi t'aeyang*, 1st ed., vol. 1, 192–94.

9. Party History Institute of the Central Committee of the Workers' Party of Korea, *Brief History of the Revolutionary Activities of Comrade Kim Il Sung* (P'yŏngyang: Foreign Languages Publishing House, 1969), 53. This is consistent with the information reported in *Kŭlloja.* Kim Ŭl-jŏn, "Chosŏn Inmin Hyŏgmyŏnggun chojik 30 chunyŏn," 31.

10. Paek Pong, *Minjok ŭi t'aeyang Kim Il Sung Changgun* [General Kim Il Sung the sun of the nation], 2nd ed., 3 vols. (P'yŏngyang: Inmun Kwahaksa, 1971, 1976, and 1976), vol. 3, 486.

11. Ibid., vol. 1, 207.

12. Suh, *Kim Il Sung*, 17.

13. Paek, *Minjok ŭi t'aeyang*, 1st ed., vol. 1, 194–95.

14. Im Ch'un-ch'u, *Hangil mujaeng t'ujaeng sigirŭl hoesang hayŏ* [Recollecting the times of the anti-Japanese armed struggle] (P'yŏngyang: Chosŏn Nodongdang Ch'ulp'ansa, 1960), 130. Henderson states that Kim Il Sung's division was initially numbered the 3rd Division of the Second Army. Gregory Henderson, *Korea: The Politics of the Vortex* (Cambridge: Harvard University Press, 1968), 325.

15. Im, *Hangil mujaeng t'ujaeng*, 130; Pak Tal, *Choguk ŭn saengmyŏng poda tŏ kwijung hada* [The fatherland is more precious than life] (P'yŏngyang: Minch'ŏng Ch'ulp'ansa, 1960), 29.

16. Im points out that Wei Zhengmin, the political commissar of the Second Army of the NEAJUA, directed the organization of the FRA. Official North Korean historiography would have the reader believe that Kim Il Sung initiated the formation of this organization. See Im, *Hangil mujaeng t'ujaeng*, 130. Suh provides an alternative view stating that Chŏn Kwang, Kim Il Sung's superior officer in the NEAJUA, formed the FRA on 10 June 1936, one month later than recorded. Suh, *Kim Il Sung*, 35.

17. Paek, *Minjok ŭi t'aeyang*, 1st ed., vol. 1, 200.

18. *Facts about Korea*, 28.

19. Suh, *Kim Il Sung*, 15–21.

20. Lim Ŭn [Hŏ Chin], *The Founding of a Dynasty in North Korea: An Authentic Biography of Kim Il-sŏng* (Tokyo: Jiyu-sha, 1982), 74–76; Suh, *Kim Il Sung*, 16, 20, 25–27.

21. The First Route Army was established on 11 May 1938 and operated in southern Manchuria; the Second Route Army was organized in January 1937 and operated in eastern Manchuria; the Third Route Army was organized in 1936 and operated in northern Manchuria. Suh, *Kim Il Sung*, 18.

22. Henderson, *Korea*, 325.

23. Lim, *Founding of a Dynasty*, 78–79.

24. Suh relates a combined battle where the forces of Kim Il Sung and Ch'oe Hyŏn joined together to raid the outpost of Yokoyama Timber Camp on 9 June 1937. This battle, which occurred directly after Kim's raid at Poch'ŏnbo and Ch'oe's battle at Munsan, resulted in nineteen Japanese casualties and earned Kim notoriety among the Japanese. Suh, *Kim Il Sung*, 35.

25. Kim Il Sung provided this bounty figure to Anna Louise Strong during her interview with him in 1947. Anna Louise Strong, "I Saw the North Koreans," An Address, 16 July 1950 (Harvard College Library, Cambridge), 7. Suh states that in 1939 Kim's bounty was 200,000 yen. Suh, *Kim Il Sung*, 30.

26. Suh, *Kim Il Sung*, 24.

27. Ibid., 48.

28. Nam Koon Woo, *The North Korean Communist Leadership, 1945–1965: A Study of Factionalism and Political Consolidation* (*Tuscaloosa*: University of Alabama Press, 1974), 43–45.

29. O Chung Chin, "The Government and Power Structure of North Korea," in *Government and Politics of Korea*, ed. Se-Jin Kim (Silver Spring, MD: Research Institute on Korean Affairs, 1972), 178; Chong-sik Lee, "Politics in North Korea: Pre-Korean War Stage" in *China Quarterly* (April–June 1963), 8.

30. U.S. Department of State, *North Korea: A Case Study in the Techniques of Take-over.* Department of State Publication No. 7118, Far Eastern Series No. 103. (Washington, DC: U.S. Government Printing Office, 1961), 115; Bruce Cumings, *Origins of the Korean War*, 2 vols. (Princeton, NJ: Princeton University Press, 1981, 1990), vol. 2, 358.

31. "Tongnip Tongmaeng kŭp Ŭiyong-gun Yoin ŭi Yakyŏk" [Short biographies of the important people of the Independence League and the Volunteer Army], in *Shin Ch'ŏn-ji* (Seoul), vol. I, no. 2 (March 1946): 238–41.

32. Cumings, *Origins of the Korean War*, vol. 2, 358.

33. Lim, *Founding of a Dynasty*, 111; Suh, *Kim Il Sung*, 20, 29.

34. Ibid.

35. Nam, *North Korean Communist Leadership*, 17.

36. Chung Kiwon, "The North Korean People's Army and the Party," *China Quarterly* (April–June 1963), 106; Nam, *North Korean Communist Leadership*, 16.

37. Han Chae-dŏk, *Kongsan chuŭi iron gwa hyŏnsil pip'an chŏnsŏ*, vol. 5, *Hanguk ŭi kongsan chuŭi wa pukhan ŭi yŏksa* [A complete critique of communism theory and reality: Korean communism and the history of North Korea] (Seoul: Naeoe Munhwasa, 1965), 129–30.

38. Paek, *Minjok ŭi t'aeyang*, 1st ed., vol. 1, 344, 346.

CHAPTER 2. BIRTH OF A NATION AND ITS ARMY

1. Charles K. Armstrong, *The North Korean Revolution, 1945–1950* (Ithaca, NY: Cornell University Press, 2003), 54.

2. Henderson, *Korea*, 17.

3. Joungwon A. Kim, *Divided Korea: The Politics of Development, 1945–1972* (Cambridge: East Asian Research Center Harvard University, 1975), 86.

4. The *Kantōgun*, or Guandong Army, derived its name from the Japanese-administered region of the Liaodong peninsula, which was renamed *Kantōshu*, or the Guandong Leased Territory, after obtaining possession of the area in 1905, a portion of the indemnity won during the

Russo-Japanese War. Owen Lattimore, *Manchuria: Cradle of Conflict* (New York: Macmillan, 1935), 30.

5. Erik Van Ree, *Socialism in One Zone: Stalin's Policy in Korea, 1945–1947* (New York: St. Martin's, 1989), 58. Van Ree provides an informative account of Soviet military action in Korea.

6. Van Ree estimates that the wartime strength of the Twenty-fifth Army was about one hundred thousand soldiers. Van Ree, *Socialism in One Zone*, 53, 62.

7. Ibid., 62–64.

8. Ibid., 91.

9. Ibid., 85.

10. Ibid., 86.

11. Cumings, *Origins of the Korean War*, vol. 1, 270.

12. Scalapino and Lee, *Communism in Korea*, part 1, 315.

13. Lim, *Founding of a Dynasty*, 123.

14. Kim Il Sung is said to have returned to Korea on the Soviet warship *Purgachov* with company commander Ch'oe Yong-jin, and Ch'oe Yong-gŏn, Kim Ch'aek, Yi Tong-hwa, Mu Il, Yu Sŏng-chŏl, Pak Kil-nam, Yi Chong-sŏng, Kim Ch'ang-guk, and Kim Paul. Lim also states that there were other Korean members of the 88th Special Brigade who returned to Korea by land, including Kang Kŏn and Kim Kwang-hyŏp. Lim, *Founding of a Dynasty*, 124.

15. Maj. Gen. Nikolai Georgievich Lebedev, a member of the Military Council of the Twenty-fifth Army from 1941 to 1947, told Suh in 1978 that Kim wore the rank of a Soviet captain. Suh, *Kim Il Sung*, 60. Compare with Han, who states that Kim told him in 1947 that he wore the rank of a Soviet major. Han, *Kongsan chuŭi iron gwa hyŏnsil pip'an chŏnsŏ*, 129–30.

16. Lim, *Founding of a Dynasty*, 125.

17. Suh Dae-Sook, "Soviet Korean and North Korea," in *Koreans in the Soviet Union*, ed. Suh Dae-Sook (Honolulu: Center for Korean Studies University of Hawaii, 1987), 107.

18. Richard E. Lauterbach, *Danger from the East* (New York: Harper & Brothers, 1947), 212.

19. Suh Dae-Sook, "A Preconceived Formula for Sovietization: North Korea," in *The Anatomy of Communist Takeovers*, ed. Thomas T. Hammond (New Haven, CT: Yale University Press, 1975), 477.

20. Philip Rudolph, *North Korea's Political and Economic Structure* (New York: International Secretariat, Institute of Pacific Relations, 1959), 26;

"Korea—The Crossroads of Korea," *Amerasia*, "Korea-The Crossroads of Korea," (October 1945): 271–77. For a different viewpoint, see Suh, "Soviet Korean and North Korea," 107.

21. Lauterbach, *Danger from the East*, 212.

22. U.S. Department of State, *North Korea*, 12. For a different viewpoint, see Lim, *Founding of a Dynasty*, 112.

23. On 3 September 1945, the day after the Japanese officially surrendered, the First Far Eastern Front was reflagged as the Maritime Military District, its peacetime unit designation. Van Ree, *Socialism in One Zone*, 102.

24. Ibid., 105.

25. Ibid., 108.

26. Kim Ch'ang-sun, *Pukhan sibonyŏnsa* [Fifteen-year history of North Korea] (Seoul: Chimungak, 1961), 190. Later two females (one Communist and one nationalist) were added to the group, increasing its total number to thirty-two people. O Yŏng-jin, *Hana ŭi chŭngŏn: sogunjŏngha ŭi pukhan [One testimony: North Korea under the Soviet military occupation]* (Pusan: Kungmin Sasang Chidowon, 1952), 24–26, 116–17.

27. Kim Il Sung, "Mokchŏn chosŏn chŏngch'i chŏngse wa pukchosŏn imshi wiwŏnhoe ŭi chosŏn e kwanhayŏ: Pukchosŏn minjujuŭi chŏngdang, sahoe tanch'e, haengjŏngguk, inmin wiwŏnhoe taep'yo hwaktae hyŏb ŭi hoe esŏ han pogo, 8 February 1946" [On the Present Political Situation in Korea and the Organization of the North Korean Interim People's Committee, 8 February 1946], in *Kim Il Sung Sŏnjip* [Selected Works of Kim Il Sung], vol. 1 (P'yŏngyang: Chosŏn Nodongdang Ch'ulp'ansa, 1963)," 43; Kim, Chang-soon, "Formation of Kim Il-sung Regime," in *North Korean Communism: A Comparative Analysis*, eds. Chong-Shik Chung and Gahb-chol Kim (Seoul: Research Center for Peace and Unification, 1980), 62.

28. Kim Ch'ang-sun, *Pukhan sibonyŏnsa*, 49–50.

29. Yŏnhap News Agency, *North Korea Handbook*, trans. Monterey Interpretation and Translation Services (Armonk, NY: M. E. Sharpe, 2003), 652.

30. O Yŏng-jin, *Hana ŭi chŭngŏn*, 141–43.

31. Kim Joungwon, *Divided Korea*, 86. According to Lim, Maj. Gen. Nikolai Georgievich Lebedev, a member of the Military Council of the Twenty-fifth Army, introduced Kim Il Sung at the assembly. Lim, *Founding of a Dynasty*, 123.

32. *Chosŏn chungang yŏn'gam* [Korean Central Almanac] (P'yŏngyang: Chosŏn Nodongdang Ch'ulp'ansa, 1950), 187–88.

33. Van Ree, *Socialism in One Zone*, 116.

34. Disagreement exists among scholars and observers as to when Kim Il Sung became the head of the North Korean Bureau of the Korean Communist Party (later renamed the North Korean Communist Party, on 17 December 1945). For accounts claiming that Kim Il Sung was party head from October 1945, see Fania Isaakovna Shabshina, "Korea: After the Second World War," in *Crisis of the Colonial System: National Liberation Struggle of the Peoples of East Asia*, ed. and trans. People's Publishing House (Bombay: Peoples Publishing House, 1951), 160; Rudolph, *North Korea's Political and Economic Structure*, 25; and Kim Ch'ang-sun, *Pukhan sibonyŏnsa*, 94–96. Kim Ch'ang-sun also states that Mu Chŏng and O Ki-sŏp were concurrently selected as second secretaries of the Party. For differing views, see Suh, *Kim Il Sung*, 71, and Kim Joungwon, *Divided Korea*, 90–91.

35. Kim Ch'ang-sun, *Pukhan sibonyŏnsa*, 63.

36. Van Ree, *Socialism in One Zone*, 114.

37. Kim Ch'ang-sun, *Pukhan sibonyŏnsa*, 61–65.

38. Scalapino and Lee, *Communism in Korea*, part 1, 334.

39. Cumings, *Origins of the Korean War*, vol. 1, 412–14.

40. Paek, *Minjok ŭi t'aeyang*, 2nd ed., vol. 2, 172. A South Korean source records the establishment of the P'yŏngyang Institute as 8 February 1946. *Hanguk chŏnjaengsa: yesŭpkyojae* [Korean War history: preview course material] (Taejŏn, Korea: Yukkun Taehak [Republic of Korea Army College], 2001), 20; Yŏnhap News Agency, Korea, *North Korea Handbook*, 652.

41. In January 1949 the P'yŏngyang Institute was renamed the Second Officers School of the People's Army. Yŏnhap News Agency, *North Korea Handbook*, 652.

42. Suh, *Kim Il Sung*, 101.

43. Cumings cites a 1946 U.S. intelligence report stating that provincial *poandae* attended a two-month course. Cumings, *Origins of the Korean War*, vol. 1, 410.

44. Youn Jong-hyun, "Kim Il Sung ŭi kunsasang" [Kim Il Sung's Military Thought], in *Pukhan Kunsaron* [Writings on North Korean military], ed. Pukhan Yonguso [North Korea Studies Research Department] (Seoul, Pukhan Yonguso 1978), 223.

45. Cumings, *Origins of the Korean War*, vol. 1, 411.

46. The *ch'ŏldo poandae* was organized on 11 January 1946. Yŏnhap News Agency, *North Korea Handbook*, 652.

47. Suk-Ho Lee, *Party-Military Relations in North Korea* (Seoul, Korea: Research Center for Peace and Unification of Korea, 1989), 78.

48. Cumings, *Origins of the Korean War*, vol. 1, 410–11.

49. Ibid.

50. Appleman, *South to the Naktong, North to the Yalu: June–November 1950*, in the series United States Army in the Korean War (Washington DC: Office of the Chief of Military History, Department of the Army, 1961), 8.

51. The Moscow Agreement is recorded in the U.S. Department of State *Bulletin* (30 December 1945), 1030. Carl Berger masterfully addresses the matter of Korean trusteeship in *Korea Knot* (Philadelphia: University of Pennsylvania Press, 1957).

52. Kim Ch'ang-sun states that the Soviets purposely established this organization with Kim Il Sung as its head in order to facilitate the withdrawal of the Soviet Civil Administration. Kim Ch'ang-sun, *Pukhan sibonyŏnsa*, 191.

53. Kim Il Sung, "Mokchŏn chosŏn chŏngch'i chŏngse," 42, 44–45. Attending parties and organizations included the Communist Party, the Democratic Party, the Korean Independence Union, the General Federation of Trade Unions, the Women's Union, the Democratic Youth League, the Peasants' Union, and the Korea-Soviet Cultural Society.

54. Kim Ch'ang-sun, *Pukhan sibonyŏnsa*, 190–91; Kim Chang-soon, "Formation of Kim Il-sung Regime," 63.

55. Jian Chen, *China's Road to the Korean War: The Making of the Sino-American Confrontation* (New York: Columbia University Press, 1994), 107.

56. Various sources cite different founding dates for this institution; however, none of these independent sources offer supporting references. May 1946 is the recorded date in *Hanguk chŏnjaengsa*, 20. The South Korean Yŏnhap News Agency reported that "In June 1946, military education institutes, such as the Security Cadre School (reorganized into the First Officers School in December 1948), were established." Yŏnhap News Agency, *North Korea Handbook*, 652. According to Paek, "in July 1946 [the Korean Communists] established a school for training the cadres of the national security forces to carry out technical training of military cadres." Paek, *Minjok ŭi t'aeyang*, 2nd ed., vol. 2, 172.

57. According to Kim Ch'ang-sun, Ch'oe Yong-gŏn left his post as the chief of the NKIPC Security Bureau between June and July 1946. Kim Ch'ang-sun, *Pukhan sibonyŏnsa*, 121, 263.

58. Kim Ch'ang-sun refers to the headquarters as the Security Cadre General Training Center (*Poan Kanbu Ch'ong Hullyŏnso*). Kim Ch'ang-sun, *Pukhan sibonyŏnsa*, 263. For differing naming sources, see Youn, "Kim Il Sung ŭi kunsasang," 223–24, and Scalapino and Lee, *Communism in Korea*, part 2, 923.

59. *Hanguk chŏnjaengsa*, 20.

60. Ibid.

61. Kim Ch'ang-sun, *Pukhan sibonyŏnsa*, 263.

62. Disagreements exist between authors and observers as to who actually served as the cultural commander. According to Kim Ch'ang-sun, Kim Il served in this capacity, but according to Scalapino and Lee it was Kim Ch'aek. It should be remembered that this portion of Scalapino and Lee's book was written from an interview with Yi Ki-gŏn, a former officer in the 1st (*Kaech'ŏn*) Division, who states that Kim Il was the political commissar for his division. Apparently, Kim Ch'aek was at least initially dual-hatted as commandant of the P'yŏngyang Institute and cultural commander of the SCGTC. It is most likely that Kim Il replaced Kim Ch'aek as political commissar when Kim Ch'aek was appointed vice chairman of the NKPC in February 1947. Scalapino and Lee, *Communism in Korea*, part 2, 923–24. Kim Ch'ang-sun, *Pukhan sibonyŏnsa*, 263.

63. Paek, *Minjok ŭi t'aeyang*, 2nd ed., vol. 2, 172; *Hanguk chŏnjaengsa*, 20.

64. Kim Ch'ang-sun lists Sinŭiju as one of the four training bases; the Republic of Korea Army College excludes Sinŭiju and includes P'yŏngyang as a training base. Kim Ch'ang-sun, *Pukhan sibonyŏnsa*, 263; *Hanguk chŏnjaengsa*, 20.

65. U.S. Department of State, *North Korea*, 85–86.

66. Scalapino and Lee, *Communism in Korea*, part 2, 925.

67. Yŏnhap News Agency, *North Korea Handbook*, 652. A contrasting account states that the aviation company was established in May 1946 and the Maritime Security Corps was established in August 1946. *Chŏk ŭl alcha (I): yŏndaegŭp isang pukkoegun chŏnsulgyori* [Understanding the enemy (volume 1): North Korean military tactical doctrine, regiment level and higher] Reference Manual 30-7-1 (Seoul: Korean Army Headquarters, 2000), 19.

68. Scalapino and Lee, *Communism in Korea*, part 2, 925.

69. *Yananist* Ch'oe Tŏk-jo apparently commanded the Chinnamp'o brigade. Cumings, *Origins of the Korean War*, vol. 2, 362.
70. Kim Ch'ang-sun, *Pukhan sibonyŏnsa*, 263; Suh, *Kim Il Sung*, 102.
71. Kim Ch'ang-sun, *Pukhan sibonyŏnsa*, 98–99.
72. The Northern Korean Bureau of the Korean Communist Party was renamed the North Korean Communist Party on 17 December 1945, during the Third Enlarged Conference of the Executive Committee of the Central Bureau. Nam, *North Korean Communist Leadership*, 25.
73. The New People's Party, or *Sinmindang*, was established on 30 March 1946 as the successor organization of the Korean Independence League. Kim Tu-bong was named chairman, and Ch'oe Ch'ang-ik and Han Sik were named vice chairmen. This party was highly favored by the *Yanan* Group. Kim Ch'ang-sun, *Pukhan sibonyŏnsa*, 97. Others, like Suh Dae-Sook, refer to the *Sinmindang* as the New Democratic Party.
74. Kim Ch'ang-sun, *Pukhan sibonyŏnsa*, 203–204.
75. Ibid., 204.
76. Ibid., 127–28.
77. Cumings, *Origins of the Korean War*, vol. 2, 362.
78. Ibid., 358–59, 363.
79. Chen, *China's Road to the Korean War*, 106.
80. Suh, *Kim Il Sung*, 102.
81. U.S. Department of State, *North Korea*, 12.
82. Ibid., 69.
83. In May 1944, according to a Japanese census, 9,170,000 people lived north of the 38th parallel and 15,944,000 people lived south of the parallel. By September 1946, South Korea's population had increased to 19,369,270, an increase of 22 percent. Most of this population increase can be attributed to a northern exodus. Assuming a direct proportional decrease in the north's population, in late 1946 North Korea would have had an approximate population of 5,744,730, plus the tens of thousands of people who relocated to Korea from China, Manchuria, and the Soviet Union. For population statistics, see Scalapino and Lee, *Communism in Korea*, part 1, 313.
84. Youn, "Kim Il Sung ŭi kunsasang," 20.
85. On 20 August 1946 the aviation company was organized as a regular unit (as opposed to a training unit). Since 1972 North Korea has commemorated this date as the official establishment of the North Korean Air Force. Yŏnhap News Agency, *North Korea Handbook*, 653.

86. Kim Il Sung, "Choguk kwa inmin ege ch'ungsirhi pongmuha nŭn in-min'gundae ŭi kanbu ga toeyŏya handa: Poan kanbu hakkyo chae 1 ki cholupsik esŏ han yŏnsŏl, 26 October 1947" [Comrades of the People's Armed Forces must devotedly serve the fatherland and the people: a speech to the first graduating class of the Security Cadre School, 26 October 1947], in *Kim Il Sung Sŏnjip* [Selected works of Kim Il Sung], vol. 1 (P'yŏngyang: Chosŏn Nodongdang Ch'ulp'ansa, 1963), 373.

87. The eight-state committee included Australia, Canada, El Salvador, France, India, Philippines, Syria, and the Ukrainian Soviet Socialist Republic. Korea, Ministry of Foreign Affairs, *Principal Documents on Korean Problem*, 97–101.

88. Ibid.

89. Kim Ch'ang-sun, *Pukhan sibonyŏnsa*, 206.

90. Ibid., 122, 266.

91. Kim Il Sung, "Chosŏn Inmin'gun ch'anggun e chehayŏ," 73, 79–80.

92. Cumings, *Origins of the Korean War*, vol. 2, 360; Suh, *Kim Il Sung*, 102.

93. Han Il-mu was a Soviet naval officer prior to returning to Korea in 1945. Suh, "Soviet Korean and North Korea," 104.

94. Chung states that An Kil was the general chief of staff when the NKPA was formed in 1948; however, An Kil died on 13 December 1947 while serving as the chief of staff for the People's Army Group. Chung, "North Korean People's Army and the Party," 108.

95. Lim, *Founding of a Dynasty*, 175.

96. Korea, Ministry of Foreign Affairs, *Principal Documents on Korean Problem*, 102–03.

97. U.S. Department of State, *North Korea*, 45.

98. Ibid., 39–43. Appleman states that the Border Constabulary had 18,500 men organized into five brigades. Appleman, *South to the Naktong*, 11.

99. Kim Ch'ang-sun, *Pukhan sibonyŏnsa*, 122.

100. Appleman, *South to the Naktong*, 8.

101. Ibid., 9.

102. U.S. Department of State, *North Korea*, 17.

103. According to interrogation reports during the Korean War, the 3rd NKPA Division was activated sometime in either February or October 1948. John Pike, "Korean People's Army," *GlobalSecurity.org* Database. Available from http://www.globalsecurity.org/military/world/dprk/army.htm. Internet accessed on 29 November 2003. Appleman states that the 3rd and 4th NKPA Divisions were created sometime between 1947 and 1949.

Appleman, *South to the Naktong*, 9. Compare with Scalapino and Lee, who mention that in 1948 the 3rd NKPA Division was a new division. Scalapino and Lee, *Communism in Korea*, part 1, 392.

104. Cumings estimates that in 1949 there were between thirty thousand and forty thousand returnees. Cumings, *Origins of the Korean War*, vol. 2, 364.

105. Kim Yong-bŏm, Correspondence with the author, Yukkun Taehak [Republic of Korea Army College], Taejŏn, Korea, January–July 2001.

106. Pike, "Korean People's Army."

107. Ibid.

108. Ibid.

109. Ibid.

110. Ibid.

111. Elliot A. Cohen and John Gooch, "Aggregate Failure: The Defeat of the American Eighth Army in Korea, November–December 1950," in *Military Misfortunes: The Anatomy of Failure in War* (New York: Free Press, 1990), 176.

112. Jonathan M. House, *Toward Combined Arms Warfare: A Survey of 20th-Century Tactics, Doctrine, and Organization*. Research Survey. U.S. Army Command and General Staff College, Combat Studies Institute no. 2, 1984, 142.

113. Ibid., 143.

114. Ibid.

115. Ibid.

116. Ibid., 147.

117. Ibid., 147–49.

118. Ibid., 149.

119. The actual number of troops in a PLA division varied greatly; hence, there is little consensus among observers as to how many personnel were authorized in a division. Samuel B. Griffith states that a PLA division had ten thousand soldiers. Robert B. Rigg estimates an authorization of about eleven thousand soldiers per division, although he states that most divisions in 1950 had only about seven thousand soldiers assigned. Li Xiaobing, Allan R. Millett, and Bin Yu estimate that a PLA division had an authorization of between thirteen thousand and fifteen thousand soldiers. Samuel B. Griffith II, *Chinese People's Liberation Army* (New York: McGraw-Hill, 1967), 131; Robert B. Rigg, *Red China's*

Fighting Hordes (Harrisburg, PA: Military Service Publishing, 1951), 63; Li Xiaobing, Allan R. Millett, and Bin Yu, trans. and eds., *Mao's Generals Remember Korea* (Lawrence: University of Kansas Press, 2001), 254.

120. Rigg, *Red China's Fighting Hordes*, 65; Cohen and Gooch, "Aggregate Failure," 176.

121. Marshal Nie Rongzhen states that in the first quarter of 1951, the PRC was able to produce only 10 percent of its munitions requirements (1,500 tons of 14,100 tons expended), compelling it to purchase 12,000 tons from foreign nations. Li, Millett, and Bin, *Mao's Generals Remember Korea*, 58.

122. Ibid., 57–58.

123. In February 1950, China and the Soviet Union signed two bilateral agreements: the "Sino-Soviet Mutual Assistance and Alliance Treaty" and the "Agreement on a Soviet Loan to the People's Republic of China." In June 1951, Marshal Xu Xiangqian, chief of the PLA General Staff, met with Col. Gen. S. M. Shtemenko, chief of General Staff of the Soviet Army, to coordinate arms purchases. During this meeting, the Soviets agreed to provide enough weapons and equipment for sixteen infantry divisions by the end of 1951 and for another forty-four divisions by the end of 1954. Ibid., 143.

124. Sun Tzu, *The Art of War*, trans. Samuel B. Griffith (Oxford: Clarendon Press, 1963), 66–69.

125. Appleman, *South to the Naktong*, 14; T. R. Fehrenbach, *This Kind of War: The Classic Korean War History* (New York: Macmillan, 1963; reprt. Dulles, VA: Brassey's, 2000), 7, 49.

126. Only four ROKA divisions—the 1st, 6th, 7th, and the Capital Division—were filled at near strength, while the 2nd, 3rd, 5th, and 8th Divisions were manned with between seven thousand and eight thousand soldiers each. Appleman, *South to the Naktong*, 15.

127. By June 1950 the ROKA had only five howitzer battalions, one each in the 1st, 2nd, 6th, 7th, and the 8th Divisions, with a sixth battalion being formed as the war started. Ibid., 16.

128. Yukkun Taehak [Republic of Korea Army College], *Hanguk chŏnjaengsa* [Korean War history: lecture], Taejŏn, Korea, 2001.

129. Appleman, *South to the Naktong*, 17.

130. Ibid.

CHAPTER 3. EXPANSION OF THE (NORTH) KOREAN PEOPLE'S ARMY

1. Kim Ch'ang-sun, *Pukhan sibonyŏnsa*, 81.

2. Appleman, *South to the Naktong*, 7.

3. *Chŏk ŭl alcha*, 35–36.

4. Mao Tse Tung (Zedong), *Selected Military Writings of Mao Tse-tung*, 2nd ed. (Beijing [Peking]: Foreign Languages Press, 1967), 212–13.

5. *Chŏk ŭl alcha*, 12–13.

6. F. F. Liu, *Military History of Modern China: 1924–1949* (Princeton, NJ: Princeton University Press, 1956), 258–60.

7. U.S. Department of State, *North Korea*, 17, 69.

8. Cumings estimates that in 1949 there were between 30,000 and 40,000 returnees. Cumings, *Origins of the Korean War*, vol. 2, 363. However, according to a U.S. Department of State report, between 20,000 and 22,000 ethnic-Korean soldiers were transferred from the PLA to the NKPA in 1949. U.S. Department of State, *North Korea*, 17.

9. U.S. Department of State, *North Korea*, 117.

10. Ibid.

11. Lim, *Founding of a Dynasty*, 175.

12. Appleman, *South to the Naktong*, 9.

13. Kim Yong-bŏm, Correspondence with the author, Yukkun Taehak.

14. The Huangpu (Whampoa) Military Academy was founded by Sun Yatsen in May 1924. Gen. Jiang Jieshi (Chiang Kai-shek) served as the academy's first president. Liu, *Military History of Modern China*, 8–9.

15. U.S. Department of State, *North Korea*, 85–86.

16. Yŏnhap News Agency, *North Korea Handbook*, 652.

17. Li, Millett, and Bin, *Mao's Generals Remember Korea*, 47–48.

18. Ibid., 47. In the 1940s, some one hundred thousand Korean residents in China joined the PLA to fight in these two wars. Chen, *China's Road to the Korean War*, 106.

19. Ibid., 48.

20. Nie, *Nie Rongzhen Huiyilu* [Nie Rongzhen's memoirs] (Beijing: People's Liberation Army Press, 1986), 743–44.

21. Chen, *China's Road to the Korean War*, 110, 255.

22. Appleman states that these soldiers numbered twelve thousand. Appleman, *South to the Naktong*, 10, 103; Cumings, *Origins of the Korean War*, vol. 2, 363.

23. Cumings, *Origins of the Korean War*, vol. 2, 363, 838.

24. U.S. Department of State, *North Korea*, 102.

25. Kim Yong-bŏm, Correspondence with the author, Yukkun Taehak.

26. Appleman, *South to the Naktong*, 10.

27. U.S. Department of State, *North Korea*, 117.

28. Ibid.

29. Appleman, *South to the Naktong*, 10.

30. Lim, *Founding of a Dynasty*, 175.

31. U.S. Department of State, *North Korea*, 45.

32. *Hanguk chŏnjaengsa*, 73.

33. Kim Yong-bŏm, Correspondence with the author, Yukkun Taehak.

34. Appleman, *South to the Naktong*, 104.

35. Kim Yong-bŏm, Correspondence with the author, Yukkun Taehak.

36. Cumings cites Gen. Douglas MacArthur's top-secret report of September 1950 and military archives from November 1950. Cumings, *Origins of the Korean War*, vol. 2, 363, 838.

37. U.S. Department of State, *North Korea*, 17, 39.

38. The 105th Armored Brigade was designated the 105th Armored Division in late June 1950, just before crossing the Han River in Seoul. Appleman, *South to the Naktong*, 10.

39. Kim Ch'ang-sun, *Pukhan sibonyŏnsa*, 266. Appleman estimates the total force size, including the NKPA and the BC, at 135,000 personnel. Appleman, *South to the Naktong*, 10; Chung estimates the force strength at between 200,000 and 300,000 personnel. Chung, "North Korean People's Army and the Party," 110.

CHAPTER 4. THE (NORTH) KOREAN PEOPLE'S ARMY OF 1950

1. Cumings, *Origins of the Korean War*, vol. 2, 446.

2. U.S. Department of State, *North Korea*, 113–14.

3. Kim Ch'ang-sun, *Pukhan sibonyŏnsa*, 266; Cumings, *Origins of the Korean War*, vol. 2, 446; Appleman, *South to the Naktong*, 8.

4. Cumings, *Origins of the Korean War*, vol. 2, 447.

CHAPTER 5. NATIONAL STRATEGY AND MILITARY POLICY FOUNDATION

1. On 28 June 1950 the ROK Army Command could account for only twenty-two thousand personnel of the ninety-eight thousand soldiers it had fielded just three days earlier, on 25 June. Fehrenbach, *This Kind of War*, 49.

2. *Chŏk ŭl alcha*, 12.

3. Republic of Korea Ministry of National Defense [ROK MND], *Kukpang Paeksŏ: 2004* [Defense White Paper: 2004] (Seoul, Korea: Ministry of National Defense, 2004), 39.
4. Ibid., 37.
5. Ibid., 39.
6. James M. Minnich, *The Denuclearization of North Korea: The Agreed Framework and Alternative Options Analyzed* (Bloomington, IN: 1st Books Library, 2002), 73.
7. Leon J. LaPorte, "Statement of General LaPorte Commander, United Nations Command; Commander, Republic of Korea-United States Combined Forces Command; and Commander, United States Forces Korea before the Senate Armed Services Committee," 8 March 2005.
8. For a thorough examination of North Korea's nuclear weapons programs, see James M. Minnich, "Resolving the North Korean Nuclear Crisis: Challenges and Opportunities in Readjusting the U.S.-ROK Alliance," in *Democratic Consolidation and Strategic Readjustment on the Korean Peninsula,*" ed. Alexander Mansourov (Honolulu: APCSS Press, 2005), and *Denuclearization of North Korea.*
9. *Chŏk ŭl alcha*, 214–15.
10. ROK MND, *Kukpang Paeksŏ: 2004*, 37.

CHAPTER 6. OFFENSIVE TACTICS

1. *Chŏk ŭl alcha* and *Chŏk chunsul* were the only source documents used and extensively referenced for this chapter.

CHAPTER 7. DEFENSIVE TACTICS

1. *Chŏk ŭl alcha* and *Chŏk chunsul* were the only source documents used and extensively referenced for this chapter.

CHAPTER 8. ARTILLERY GROUPING TACTICS

1. *Chŏk ŭl alcha* and *Chŏk chunsul* were the only source documents used and extensively referenced for this chapter.

APPENDIX A. A HISTORIC REVIEW

1. Losing the Sino-Japanese War of 1894–1895, China relinquished suzerainty over Korea after signing the Shimonoseko Treaty. Koo Young-nok, "The Conduct of Foreign Affairs," in *Korean Politics in Transition*, ed. Edward Reynolds Wright (Seattle: University of Washington Press, 1975), 209.

2. Gari Ledyard, "Yin and Yang in the China-Manchuria-Korea Triangle," in *China among Equals*, ed. Morris Rossabi (Berkeley: University of California Press, 1983), 321, 323.

3. Carter J. Eckert, Ki-baik Lee, Young Ick Lew, Michael Robinson, and Edward W. Wagner, *Korea Old and New* (Cambridge: Korea Institute, Harvard University, 1990), 91, 99.

4. Benjamin H. Hazard, "The Wakō and Korean Responses," in *Papers in Honor of Professor Woodbridge Bingham: A Festschrift for His Seventy-fifth Birthday.* James B. Parsons, ed. (San Francisco, CA: Chinese Material Center, 1976), 15; Eckert, et al., *Korea Old and New*, 100.

5. Peter Duus, *The Abacus and the Sword: The Japanese Penetration of Korea, 1895–1910* (Berkeley: University of California Press, 1995), 20.

6. Lauterbach, *Danger from the East*, 189.

7. Koo, "Conduct of Foreign Affairs," 209.

8. Henderson, *Korea*, 17.

9. Eckert, et al., *Korea Old and New*, 256.

Glossary

KOREAN WORDS

chawidae: self-defense guards

ch'iandae: security units, or public safety corps

chibchung punsan: mass and dispersion

ch'imt'u: infiltration maneuver

chinji pangŏ: area defense

ch'inwidae: bodyguards

Choguk Kwangbokhoe: Fatherland Restoration Association (FRA)

ch'ŏldo poandae: Railroad Guard forces

ch'ŏmip: thrust maneuver

Chŏngudang: Religious Party

chŏn'gukt'o ŭi yosaehwa: stronghold-based fortified country

chŏn'gun ŭi kanbuhwa: cadre-based army

chŏninmin ŭi mujanghwa: militarization of the populace

Chosŏn Inmin'gun: (North) Korean People's Army (NKPA)

Chosŏn Inmin Hyŏgmyŏnggun: Korean People's Revolutionary Army (KPRA)

Chosŏn Kŏn'guk Chunbi Wiwŏnhoe: Committee for the Preparation of Korean Independence (CPKI)

Chosŏn Ŭiyonggun: Korean Volunteer Army (KVA)

chuch'e: self-reliance

chuch'e sasang: self-reliance ideology

Chungang Poan Kanbu Hakkyo: Central Security Cadre School

Han'gil Yugyŏktae: Anti-Japanese Guerrilla Army

hullyŏnso: training center

Hwapuk Chosŏn Tongnip Tongmaeng: North Korean Interim People's Committee (NKIPC)

ilhaengch'ŏlli: Hit and Run (cunning maneuver)

imshi to wiwŏnhoe-dŭl: provisional provincial committees

Inmin Chŏngch'i Wiwŏnhoe: People's Political Committee

Inminjipdangun Ch'ongsaryŏngbu: People's Army Group General Headquarters

inmin wiwŏnhoe-dŭl: people's committees

kidongsŏng chŭngdae: increased maneuverability

kidong pangŏ: mobile defense

kimyo hago yŏnghwalhan chŏnsul: cunning and personified tactics

kisŭb chŏllyak: surprise attack

kukka mokp'yo: national objective

kunchangbi ŭi hyŏndaehwa: military equipment modernization

kunsa chŏllyak: military strategy

kunsa chŏngch'aek: military policy

kunsa sasang: military ideology

kyŏngbitae: Border Constabulary (BC)

kyŏnje: holding maneuver

mangwŏnchŏnsul: Instigate Fratricide (cunning maneuver)

Naemusŏng: Ministry of Internal Affairs

paehap chŏllyak: mixed tactics

pangŏ chŏnsul: defensive tactics

pimil pojang: secure secrets

p'och'o: besetment maneuver

poandae: peace preservation corps, police

Poan Kanbu Ch'ong Hullyŏnso: Security Cadre General Training Center (SCGTC)

Poan Kanbu Hullyŏn Taedae Ponbu: Security Cadre's Training Battalion Headquarters

Poankuk: Security Bureau

p'owi: encirclement maneuver

Powiguk: National Defense Bureau

Powisŏng: Ministry of National Defense (MND)

Pukchosŏn Nodongdang: North Korean Workers' Party (NKWP)

Pukchosŏn Odo Haengjŏngguk: Five North Korean Provinces' Administrative Bureau (FNKPAB)

sadae kunsanosŏn: Four-Point Military Guideline

Samp'al Kyŏngbi Yŏdan: 38th Constabulary Brigade

Sinmindang: New People's Party

sobudae: special operations force teams

sobudae hwaltong: small-unit activities

sojwa: military rank of major

sokchŏn sokkyŏl chŏllyak: quick, decisive war strategy

taebudae: regular combat forces

tolp'a: penetration maneuver

tongkyŏksŏsŭb: East Strike West Attack (cunning maneuver)

tongsŏngsŏkyŏk: East Sound West Attack (cunning maneuver)

uhoe: turning maneuver

ŭibyŏng: Righteous Armies

wŏn chunch'ik: principles of war

Yi Hong-gwang Chidae: Yi Hong-gwang Detachment (YHD)

JAPANESE WORDS

Kantōgun: Guandong or Kwantung Army

kokui: national prestige

tōkan: resident-general

tōkanfu: residency-general

Wakō: Japanese pirates

RUSSIAN WORDS

komendatura: local commander bureau

CHINESE WORDS

Dongbei Kangri Lianjun: Northeast Anti-Japanese United Army (NEAJUA)

Guomindang: Nationalist Party

Annotated Bibliography

Amerasia, "Korea-The Crossroads of Korea," (October 1945): 271–277.

Appleman, Roy E. *South to the Naktong, North to the Yalu: June–November 1950.* In the series United States Army in the Korean War. Washington, DC: Office of the Chief of Military History, Department of the Army, 1961. [An authoritative account of the first six months of the Korean War, providing an informative insight into the military aspects of the war.]

Armstrong, Charles K. *The North Korean Revolution, 1945–1950.* Ithaca, NY: Cornell University Press, 2003. [Professor Armstrong examines the genesis of the DPRK as an example of a Communist state and as a part of modern Korean history. His account is based largely on "Record Group 242, National Archives Collection of Foreign Records Seized in 1941," which is a collection of documents that were captured by U.S. forces during the Korean War.]

Baik Bong. *Kim Il Sung: Biography.* 3 vols. Tokyo: Miraisha, 1969, 1970, and 1970. Baik Bong is Kim Il Sung's official biographer. [This three-volume edition is a translation of Paek Pong's original work *Minjok ŭi t'aeyang Kim Il Sung Changgun* (General Kim Il Sung the sun of the nation).]

Berger, Carl. *The Korea Knot.* Philadelphia: University of Pennsylvania Press, 1957.

Bush, George W. *The President's State of the Union Address.* Washington, DC: The White House, 2002. Database. Available from http://www.whitehouse.gov. Internet accessed on 11 March 2002.

Central Intelligence Agency. "The World Factbook—Korea, North." *CIA.gov.* Available from http://www.cia.gov Internet accessed on 11 March 2002.

Chen Jian. *China's Road to the Korean War: The Making of the Sino-American Confrontation.* New York: Columbia University Press, 1994. [Professor Chen Jian of Southern Illinois University traveled to China in 1987, 1991, 1992, and 1993 where he interviewed many Chinese scholars and accessed many original source materials, which serve as the basis for this study.]

Chŏk ŭl alcha (I): yŏndaegŭp isang pukkoegun chŏnsulgyori [Understanding the enemy (volume 1): North Korean military tactical doctrine, regiment level and higher] Reference Manual 30-7-1. Seoul: Korean Army Headquarters, 2000. [A South Korean military manual that details North Korea's military tactical doctrine.]

Chosŏn chungang yŏn'gam [Korean Central Almanac]. P'yŏngyang: Chosŏn Nodongdang Ch'ulp'ansa, 1950.

"Chosŏn Ŭiyong-gun Ch'ong Saryŏng Mu Chŏng Changgun Ildaeki" [Biography of General Mu Chŏng, supreme commander of the Korean Volunteer Army]. *Shin Ch'ŏn-ji* (Seoul), vol. I, no. 2 (March 1946): 238–41.

Chung Kiwon. "The North Korean People's Army and the Party." *The China Quarterly* (April–June 1963), 105–24.

Cohen, Elliot A., and John Gooch. "Aggregate Failure: The Defeat of the American Eighth Army in Korea, November–December 1950." In *Military Misfortunes: The Anatomy of Failure in War.* New York: Free Press, 1990.

Cumings, Bruce. *The Origins of the Korean War,* 2 vols. Princeton, NJ: Princeton University Press, 1981, 1990.

Duus, Peter. *The Abacus and the Sword: The Japanese Penetration of Korea, 1895–1910.* Berkeley: University of California Press, 1995. [*The Abacus and the Sword* disaggregates Japan's imperialist coalition—the political from the economic—and illuminates, from the Japanese perspective, the motivations behind Japan's penetration of Korea from 1895 to 1910.]

Eckert, Carter J., Ki-baik Lee, Young Ick Lew, Michael Robinson, and Edward W. Wagner. *Korea Old and New: A History.* Cambridge: Korea Institute, Harvard University, 1990.

Facts about Korea. P'yŏngyang: Foreign Languages Publishing House, 1961. [An almanac on North Korea.]

Fehrenbach T. R. *This Kind of War: The Classic Korean War History.* New York: Macmillan, 1963. Reprint, Dulles, VA: Brassey's, 2000.

Griffith, Samuel B. II. *The Chinese People's Liberation Army.* New York: McGraw-Hill, 1967. [Brigadier General Griffith, a former U.S. Marine Corps officer who was stationed in China during the Chinese civil war, provides a fascinating history of the PLA.]

Han Chae-dŏk, *Kongsan chuŭi iron gwa hyŏnsil pip'an chŏnsŏ*. Vol. 5, *Hanguk ŭi kongsan chuŭi wa pukhan ŭi yŏksa* [A complete critique of communism theory and reality: Korean communism and the history of North Korea] Seoul: Naeoe Munhwasa, 1965. [A former North Korean journalist for the North Korean newspaper *Minju Chosŏn*. Han Chae-dŏk had personal contacts with Kim Il Sung post-1945. Han later defected to South Korea several years before his death in 1970.]

Hanguk chŏnjaengsa: yesŭpkyojae [Korean War history: preview course material] Taejŏn, Korea: Yukkun Taehak [Republic of Korea Army College], 2001. [Study material used at the Korea Army College.]

Hanguk chŏnjaengsa: poch'unggyojae [Korean War history: supplemental course material] Taejŏn, Korea: Yukkun Taehak [Republic of Korea Army College], 2001. [Study material used at the Korea Army College.]

Hazard, Benjamin H. "The Wakō and Korean Responses." In *Papers in Honor of Professor Woodbridge Bingham: A Festschrift for His Seventy-fifth Birthday*. James B. Parsons, ed. San Francisco, CA: Chinese Material Center, 1976.

Henderson, Gregory. *Korea: The Politics of the Vortex*. Cambridge: Harvard University Press, 1968.

House, Jonathan M. *Toward Combined Arms Warfare: A Survey of 20th-Century Tactics, Doctrine, and Organization*. Research Survey. U.S. Army Command and General Staff College, Combat Studies Institute no. 2, 1984.

Im Ch'un-ch'u. *Hangil mujaeng t'ujaeng sigirŭl hoesang hayŏ* [Recollecting the times of the anti-Japanese armed struggle]. P'yŏngyang: Chosŏn Nodongdang Ch'ulp'ansa, 1960. [Kim Il Sung's subordinate in the Northeast Anti-Japanese United Army chronicles many experiences from this period. In Im's recollections, he states that Kim Il Sung's superior officer, Wei Zhengmin, directed the founding of the Fatherland Restoration Association (FRA) and the Korean People's Revolutionary Army (KPRA), rather than Kim himself. As a result, this book became one of many that were later banned in North Korea.]

Kim Chang-soon. "Formation of Kim Il-sung Regime." In *North Korean Communism: A Comparative Analysis*, eds. Chong-Shik Chung and Gahb-chol Kim, 9–78. Seoul: Research Center for Peace and Unification, 1980.

Kim Ch'ang-sun. *Yŏksa ŭi chŭng-in* [The Witness of History]. Seoul: Hanguk asea pankong yŏn-maeng, 1956.

————. *Pukhan sibonyŏnsa* [Fifteen-year history of North Korea]. Seoul: Chimungak, 1961. [Kim Ch'ang-sun is a former communist reporter who used his personal insights to provide a political history of North Korea from 1945 to 1960. Additionally, he was the Director of the Institute for North Korean Studies, in South Korea.]

Kim Il Sung. "Choguk kwa inmin ege ch'ungsirhi pongmuha nŭn inmin'gundae ŭi kanbu ga toeyŏya handa: Poan kanbu hakkyo chae 1 ki cholupsik esŏ han yŏnsŏl, 26 October 1947" [Comrades of the People's Armed Forces must devotedly serve the fatherland and the people: a speech to the first graduating class of the Security Cadre School, 26 October 1947]. In *Kim Il Sung Sŏnjip* [Selected works of Kim Il Sung], vol. 1. P'yŏngyang: Chosŏn Nodongdang Ch'ulp'ansa, 1963.

————. "Chosŏn Inmin'gun ch'anggun e chehayŏ: Chosŏn Inmin'gun yŏlbyŏngsik esŏ han yŏnsŏl, 8 February 1948" [On the occasion of the creation of the Korean People's Army: speech delivered at a review of the Korean People's Army, 8 February 1948]. In *Kim Il Sung Sŏnjip* [Selected works of Kim Il Sung], vol. 2. P'yŏngyang: Chosŏn Nodongdang Ch'ulp'ansa, 1964.

————. "Chosŏn Inmin'gun ŭn hangil mujaeng t'ujaeng ŭi kyaesŭngja ida: Chosŏn Inmin'gun 324 kunbudae kwanha changbyŏngeŭl ap esŏ han yŏnsŏl, *8 February 1958*" [The Korean People's Army is the Successor to the Anti-Japanese Armed Struggle: Speech Delivered before the Officers and Men of the 324th Army Unit of the Korean People's Army, 8 February 1958]. In *Kim Il Sung Sŏnjip* [Selected Works of Kim Il Sung], vol. 5. P'yŏngyang: Chosŏn Nodongdang Ch'ulp'ansa, 1960.

————. "Mokchŏn chosŏn chŏngch'i chŏngse wa pukchosŏn imshi wiwŏnhoe ŭi chosŏn e kwanhayŏ: Pukchosŏn minjujuŭi chŏngdang, sahoe tanch'e, haengjŏngguk, inmin wiwŏnhoe taep'yo hwaktae hyŏb ŭi hoe esŏ han pogo, 8 February 1946" [On the Present Political Situation in Korea and the Organization of the North Korean Interim People's Committee, 8 February 1946]. In *Kim Il Sung Sŏnjip* [Selected Works of Kim Il Sung], vol. 1. P'yŏngyang: Chosŏn Nodongdang Ch'ulp'ansa, 1963.

Kim Joungwon A. *Divided Korea: The Politics of Development, 1945–1972*. Cambridge: East Asian Research Center, Harvard University, 1975.

"Kim Tu-bong Chusŏk ŭi T'ujaeng-sa" [Record of the struggle of Chairman Kim Tu-bong]. *Shin Ch'ŏn-ji* (Seoul), vol. I, no. 2 (March 1946): 205–07.

Kim Ŭl-jŏn. "Chosŏn Inmin Hyŏgmyŏnggun chojik 30 chunyŏn" [The 30th anniversary of the organization of the Korean People's Revolutionary Army]. *Kŭlloja* [The Worker] 244 (March 1964): 31–35.

Kim Yong-bŏm. Correspondence with the author, Yukkun Taehak [Republic of Korea Army College]. Taejŏn, Korea. January–July 2001. [A Korean Army Lieutenant Colonel and North Korean Military Tactics Instructor at the Korea Army College in Taejŏn, Korea, in 2001.]

Koo Youngnok. "The Conduct of Foreign Affairs." In *Korean Politics in Transition*, ed. Edward Reynolds Wright. Seattle: University of Washington Press, 1975.

Korea, Ministry of Foreign Affairs, comp., *Principal Documents on Korean Problem, 1943–1960*, vol. 1. Seoul, 1960. [A comprehensive collection of English-language official documents, bearing relevance on the "Korean Problem."]

Korean Revolutionary Museum. P'yŏngyang: Foreign Languages Publishing House, 1963. [This book depicts the fifteen exhibit rooms of the Korean Revolutionary Museum, in P'yŏngyang; for the purpose of providing a written and pictorial account of Korea's revolutionary struggle beginning with the 1884 *Kapsin Ch'ŏngbyŏn* (*coup d'état*) until national liberation in 1945, as recounted by the North Korean Workers' Party.

Kukchae yŏnhap kunjŏnsa: Naktonggang esŏ amnokkang kkachi [UN military war history: From the Naktong River to the Amnok River]. Pamphlet 70-17-1. Seoul: Yukkun ponbu [Army Headquarters], 1963. [This volume is a Korean translation of Roy E. Appleman's book *South to the Naktong, North to the Yalu: June–November 1950.*]

LaPorte, Leon J. "Statement of General Leon J. LaPorte Commander, United Nations Command; Commander, Republic of Korea-United States Combined Forces Command; and Commander, United States Forces Korea before the Senate Armed Services Committee." 8 March 2005. [This statement was written by Major James M. Minnich, while serving as the J5 Policy Branch chief for United States Forces Korea.]

Lattimore, Owen. *Manchuria: Cradle of Conflict.* New York: Macmillan, 1935.

Lauterbach, Richard E. *Danger from the East.* New York: Harper & Brothers, 1947. [Principally a survey of East Asia during the post–World War II era. Regarding Korea, it is an account of the military governments' civil administration on both sides of the thirty-eighth parallel.]

Ledyard, Gari. "Yin and Yang in the China-Manchuria-Korea Triangle." In *China among Equals*, ed. Morris Rossabi, 313–53. Berkeley: University of California Press, 1983.

Lee Chong-sik. "Korean Communists and Yenan," *The China Quarterly*, no. 9 (January–March 1962), 182–192.

————. "Politics in North Korea: Pre-Korean War Stage." *The China Quarterly* (April–June 1963), 3–16.

Lee Suk-Ho. *Party-Military Relations in North Korea.* Seoul, Korea: Research Center for Peace and Unification of Korea, 1989.

Li Xiaobing, Allan R. Millett, and Bin Yu, trans. and eds. *Mao's Generals Remember Korea.* Lawrence: University of Kansas Press, 2001. [A mosaic of memoirs by key Chinese military commanders from the Korean War.]

Lim Ŭn [Hŏ Chin]. *The Founding of a Dynasty in North Korea: An Authentic Biography of Kim Il-sŏng.* Tokyo: Jiyu-sha, 1982. Translated from *A Secret History of the Founding of a North Korean Dynasty* (in Japanese). [Lim Ŭn, a Soviet-Korean who participated in North Korean politics, wrote from exile in the former Soviet Union about the "true nature" of Kim Il Sung.]

Liu, F. F. *A Military History of Modern China: 1924–1949.* Princeton, NJ: Princeton University Press, 1956. [F. F. Liu was formerly an officer in the Chinese Nationalist forces during World War II. He came to the United States and received his doctorate at Princeton University.]

Mao Tse Tung (Zedong). *Selected Military Writings of Mao Tse-tung*, 2nd ed. Beijing (Peking): Foreign Languages Press, 1967.

Matray, James I., ed. *Historical Dictionary of the Korean War.* New York: Greenwood Press, 1991. [This descriptive essay covers the significant people, controversies, military operations, and policy pronouncements of the Korean War.]

Minnich, James M. *The Denuclearization of North Korea: The Agreed Framework and Alternative Options Analyzed.* Bloomington, Indiana: 1st Books Library, 2002. [Unique among other principal accounts of the North Korea nuclear crisis, this book analyzes four different policy options for achieving the permanent or long-term denuclearization of North Korea, including the Agreed Framework, an Amended Framework Option, a Comprehensive Framework Option, and a Coercive Denuclearization Options. However, Minnich finds that none of these prevalent and publicly debated policy options are calculated to achieve the denuclearization of North Korea.]

————. "Resolving the North Korean Nuclear Crisis: Challenges and Opportunities in Readjusting the U.S.-ROK Alliance," In *Democratic Consolidation and Strategic Readjustment on the Korean Peninsula*," ed. Alexander Mansourov, chapter 14. Honolulu: APCSS Press, 2005. [This chapter begins by examining the questions, "What are America's interests, vis-à-vis North Korea" and "What should America be willing to do to ensure the integrity of its interests" Next, Minnich examines the factors that determine which approach—unilateral or multilateral—is more appropriate to pursue policy objectives relating to the denuclearization of North Korea. Lastly, Minnich examines the U.S. and ROK policies toward a nuclear North Korea and offers a six-step process for resolving the crisis.]

Nam Koon Woo. *The North Korean Communist Leadership, 1945–1965: A Study of Factionalism and Political Consolidation.* Tuscaloosa: University of Alabama Press, 1974.

Nie Rongzhen. *Nie Rongzhen huiyilu* [Nie Rongzhen's memoirs]. Beijing: People's Liberation Army Press, 1986.

———. "Beijing's Decision to Intervene" (A translated excerpt from *Nie Rongzhen huiyilu* [Nie Rongzhen's memoirs]). Li Xiaobing, Allan R. Millett, and Bin Yu, trans. and eds. *Mao's Generals Remember Korea.* Lawrence: University of Kansas Press, 2001.

Nodong Sinmun (Workers' Daily), (P'yŏngyang)

O Chung Chin. "The Government and Power Structure of North Korea." In *Government and Politics of Korea*, ed. Se-Jin Kim, 176–202. Silver Spring, MD: Research Institute on Korean Affairs, 1972.

O Yŏng-jin, *Hana ŭi chŭngŏn: sogunjŏngha ŭi pukhan* [One testimony: North Korea under the Soviet military occupation]. Pusan: Kungmin Sasang Chidowon, 1952. [O Yŏng-jin, a former secretary of Korean nationalist Cho Man-sik, provides a personal chronicle of his experiences, including several conversations with Kim Il Sung.]

Ogata, Sadako N. *Defiance in Manchuria: The Making of Japanese Foreign Policy, 1931–1932.* Berkeley: University of California Press, 1964. [Many authentic Guandong Army documents and personal memorandums were used extensively in writing this detailed account of the Japanese annexation of Manchuria.]

Paek Pong. *Minjok ŭi t'aeyang Kim Il Sung Changgun* [General Kim Il Sung the sun of the nation], 1st ed., 2 vols. P'yŏngyang: Inmun Kwahaksa, 1968, and 1969. [An official biography of Kim Il-sung, issued by the Korean Workers' Party, which covers his life through 1967.]

———. *Minjok ŭi t'aeyang Kim Il Sung Changgun* [General Kim Il Sung the sun of the nation], 2nd ed., 3 vols. P'yŏngyang: Inmun Kwahaksa, 1971, 1976, and 1976. [The author states that he was dissatisfied with the quality of the first edition, so he republished Kim Il Sung's biography in this three-volume edition. Differences between the two additions include some factual alterations along with a succession of exalting platitudes that precede mention of Kim Il Sung's name. Additionally, volume three was published in 1971, while volumes one and two were each published in 1976.]

Pak Tal. *Choguk ŭn saengmyŏng poda tŏ kwijung hada* [The fatherland is more precious than life]. P'yŏngyang: Minch'ŏng Ch'ulp'ansa, 1960. [An autobiography by Pak Tal (1910–1960). An associate of Kim Il Sung, in 1935 Pak Tal co-organized (with Pak Kŭm-chŏl) the Kapsan Operation Committee, a Communist organization, which he reorganized in 1937 as the Korean National Liberation Union as directed by Kim Il Sung.]

Party History Institute of the Central Committee of the Workers' Party of Korea. *Brief History of the Revolutionary Activities of Comrade Kim Il Sung.* P'yŏngyang: Foreign Languages Publishing House, 1969.

People's Publishing House, LTD., ed. and trans. *Crisis of the Colonial System: National Liberation Struggle of the Peoples of East Asia.* Bombay: Peoples Publishing House, Ltd., 1951. [This volume contains reports by Soviet Academicians to the Pacific Institute of the Academy of Sciences, USSR, in 1949. Originally written in Russian and published in Moscow, the reports in this volume were translated in English and published in India by the People's Publishing House, Ltd.]

Pike, John. "Korean People's Army." *GlobalSecurity.org* Database. Available from http://www.globalsecurity.org/military/world/dprk/army.htm. Internet accessed on 29 November 2003.

Republic of Korea Ministry of National Defense. *Kukpang Paeksŏ: 2004* [Defense White Paper: 2004]. Seoul, Korea: Ministry of National Defense, 2004.

Rigg, Robert B. *Red China's Fighting Hordes.* Harrisburg, PA: Military Service Publishing Company, 1951. [Lieutenant Colonel Rigg of the U.S. military was a prisoner of the PLA during the Chinese civil war in 1947. Using various sources, including General Lin Biao's book on "Short Tactics," Rigg's text characterizes the PLA, its commanders, organizations, tactics, and strengths and weaknesses.]

Rudolph, Philip. *North Korea's Political and Economic Structure.* New York: International Secretariat, Institute of Pacific Relations, 1959. [An analysis of how the Communist system was applied to North Korea through an examination of the development of major political and economic institutions in North Korea since 1945.]

Scalapino, Robert A., and Chong-sik Lee, *Communism in Korea.* 2 vols. Berkeley: University of California Press, 1972. [In 1972 Robert Scalapino and Chong-sik Lee published a two-volume seminal work titled *Communism in Korea.* A portion of this book, which was particularly relevant to this study, examines the origins of the NKPA through the recollections of Yi Ki-gŏn as recorded in an interview with Chong-sik Lee in 1969. Yi Ki-gŏn was a Korean native who trained at the Manchukuo Military Academy before national liberation. A lieutenant colonel in the 1st NKPA Division, he defected to South Korea in 1948. For more on Yi Ki-gŏn's life, see Robert A. Scalapino and Chong-sik Lee, *Communism in Korea*, part 2, *The Society* (Berkeley: University of California Press, 1972), 921–25.]

Scalapino, Robert A., ed. *North Korea Today.* New York: Praeger, 1963. Originally published in Great Britain in 1963 as a special issue of *The China Quarterly.*

Shabshina, Fania Isaakovna. "Korea: After the Second World War." In *Crisis of the Colonial System: National Liberation Struggle of the Peoples of East Asia*, ed. and trans. People's Publishing House, LTD., 155–209. Bombay: Peoples Publishing House, Ltd., 1951. [From 1940 to 1946, Anatolii Ivanovich Shabshina was assigned to the Soviet mission in Seoul, Korea as vice-consul; he later became a deputy political advisor in North Korea. Accompanied by his wife, Fania Isaakovona Shabshina concurrently worked in the Soviet Consulate General office in Seoul and later went on to become a renowned Soviet Koreanologist.]

Simmons, Robert R. *The Strained Alliance: Peking, Pyongyang, Moscow, and the Politics of the Korean Civil War.* New York: Free Press, 1975.

Strong, Anna Louise. "I Saw the North Koreans." An Address, 16 July 1950. Harvard College Library, Cambridge. [Anna Louise Strong is an American reporter who spent three weeks in the summer of 1947 inside North Korea. In this address, she relates her affinity toward the North Koreans and her disdain for the United States' handling of Korea, particularly the Korean War.]

Suh Dae-Sook. *Kim Il Sung: The North Korean Leader.* New York: Columbia University Press, 1988. [A well-sourced, dispassionate examination of Kim Il Sung's life.]

———. *The Korean Communist Movement, 1918–1948.* Princeton, NJ: Princeton University Press, 1967. [The first English-language work on this subject using extensive primary source materials.]

———. "A Preconceived Formula for Sovietization: North Korea." In *The Anatomy of Communist Takeovers*, ed. Thomas T. Hammond, 475–89. New Haven, CT: Yale University Press, 1975.

———. "Soviet Korean and North Korea." In *Koreans in the Soviet Union*, ed. Suh Dae-Sook, 101–28. Honolulu: Center for Korean Studies University of Hawaii, 1987.

Sun Tzu, *The Art of War.* Translated by Samuel B. Griffith. Oxford: Clarendon Press, 1963.

"Tongnip Tongmaeng kŭp Ŭiyong-gun Yoin ŭi Yakyŏk" [Short biographies of the important people of the Independence League and the Volunteer Army]. *Shin Ch'ŏn-ji* (Seoul), vol. I, no. 2 (March 1946): 242–44.

U.S. Congress, Senate. "Testimony of R. James Woolsey, Hearing before the Senate Committee on Governmental Affairs." 103 Congress, 1 Session. Washington, DC: U.S. Government Printing Office, 24 February 1993.

U.S. Department of State. *North Korea: A Case Study in the Techniques of Take-over.* Department of State Publication No. 7118, Far Eastern Series No. 103. Washington, DC: U.S. Government Printing Office, 1961.

———. *Bulletin.* 30 December 1945. [An official record of the Moscow Agreement of 1945.]

Van Ree, Erik. *Socialism in One Zone: Stalin's Policy in Korea, 1945–1947.* New York: St. Martin's, 1989. [Using newly released former Soviet sources, Van Ree provides an informative account of the Soviet military's actions in Korea from 1945 to 1947.]

Yi Na-yŏng. *Chosŏn minjok haebang t'ujaengsa* [A history of the Korean People's struggle for emancipation]. P'yŏngyang: Chosŏn Nodongdang Ch'ulp'ansa, 1958. [A Communist history of the subject with emphasis on Kim Il Sung's partisan operations.]

Yŏnhap News Agency, Korea. *North Korea Handbook.* Translated by Monterey Interpretation and Translation Services. Armonk, NY: M. E. Sharpe, 2003. [An encyclopedic examination of North Korea, its history and politics.]

Youn Jong-hyun. "Kim Il Sung ŭi kunsasang" [Kim Il Sung's Military Thought], in *Pukhan Kunsaron* [Writings on North Korean military], ed. Pukhan Yonguso (Seoul, 1978).

Yu Maochun. *OSS in China: Prelude to Cold War.* New Haven, CT: Yale University Press, 1996. [This book, which is largely based on U.S. National Archive's Record Group 226, the recently declassified records of the Office of Strategic Services (OSS), is a history of the OSS in China during the 1940s.]

Yukkun Taehak [Republic of Korea Army College]. *Chŏk chunsul* [Enemy Tactics]. Taejŏn, Korea, 2001.

———. *Hanguk chŏnjaengsa: kang-ŭi* [Korean War history: lecture]. Taejŏn, Korea, 2001. [While attending the Korea Army College from January to July 2001, I collected many notes and documents that remain in my possession, including many briefing slides on the history of the Korean War.]

Index

Page numbers followed by *n*, plus a number, refer to endnotes.

FNKPAB. *See* Five North Korean
Provinces' Administrative Bureau
*The Founding of a Dynasty in North
Korea: An Authentic Biography of
Kim Il-sŏng* (Lim Ŭn), 5
Four-Point Military Guideline,
69–71
FRA. *See* Fatherland Restoration
Association

general observation post (GOP), 82
general security outpost (GSOP), 92
GOP. *See* general observation post
GSOP. *See* general security outpost
Guandong Army. *See Kantōgun*
guerrilla combat techniques, 16–17,
54, 74
Gulf War (1991), lessons from,
67–68
Guomindang, 142

Han Chae-dŏk, 5, 19
Han Il-mu, 36, 131n93
Han Kyŏng, 59
Han Pin, 18
*Hangil mujaeng t'uaeng sigirŭl
hoe-sang hayŏ* (Im Ch'un-ch'u), 4
Han'gil Yugyŏktae, 140
*Hanguk ŭi kongsan chŭi wa pukhan
ŭi yŏsa* (Han Chae-dŏk), 5
Henan Military Academy, 18
Hepburn transliteration system, 7
holding maneuver, 83–84
hullyŏnso, 140
hullyŏnso-dŭl, 30
*Hwapuk Chosŏn Tongnip
Tongmaeng*, 140
Hŏ Ka-i, 19

ilhaengch'ŏlli, 140
Im Ch'un-ch'u, 4
Imjin War, 110
imshi to wiwŏnhoe-dŭl, 140
inclement weather, 77
infiltration maneuver, 84–85
Inmin Chŏngch'i Wiwŏnhoe, 140
inmin wiwŏnhoe-dŭl, 140
Inminjipdangun Ch'ongsaryŏngbu,
35, 140
integrated fire support, 101
Internal Affairs Bureau, 34, 36
Itō Hirobumi, 112

Japan: expansion in Korea,
110–12; Korea annexed by, 112;
Korean liberation from, 2;
Manchuria annexed by, 12;
occupation by, 2; raids on Korea,
110
Japanese: guerilla war, 1; Kim Il
Sung's reputation among,
123n24; Seventeenth Front of, 22
Jiang Jiesh (Chian Kai-shek), 34

Kang Kŏn, xvi, 19, 32, 37, 57
Kanggye Artillery Regiment, 33
Kantōgun, 12, 22, 141: name
derivation of, 124n4; NEAJUA
defeated by, 17
"Kapsan faction," 12
Kapsan Operation Committee, 31.
See also Korean National
Liberation Union
Kapsan partisans, 12, 59; origins of,
2
Kapsanists, 24, 59; as core leaders
of North Korea armed forces, 32;

About the Author

James M. Minnich is a United States Army Foreign Area Officer currently serving as the J5 Policy Branch chief in the United States Forces Korea (USFK). Since 1982 he has served numerous military assignments in Korea. His academic degrees include an Artium Magister (MA) in East Asian Studies from Harvard University's Graduate School of Arts and Sciences and a Master in Military Art and Science (MMAS) from the United States Army Command and General Staff College. Additionally, he is an alumnus of the Republic of Korea Army College in Taejŏn, South Korea, and Sŏgang University's Center for Korean Studies in Seoul, South Korea. His previous publications include *The Denuclearization of North Korea: The Agreed Framework and Alternative Policy Options Analyzed* (2002); "Resolving the North Korean Nuclear Crisis: Challenges and Opportunities in Readjusting the U.S.-ROK Alliance," in *Democratic Consolidation and Strategic Readjustment on the Korean Peninsula* (2005); and articles and book reviews that have appeared in *The Korean Journal of Defense Analyses* and the *F.A.O. Journal*.

The **Naval Institute Press** is the book-publishing arm of the U.S. Naval Institute, a private, nonprofit, membership society for sea service professionals and others who share an interest in naval and maritime affairs. Established in 1873 at the U.S. Naval Academy in Annapolis, Maryland, where its offices remain today, the Naval Institute has members worldwide.

Members of the Naval Institute support the education programs of the society and receive the influential monthly magazine *Proceedings* and discounts on fine nautical prints and on ship and aircraft photos. They also have access to the transcripts of the Institute's Oral History Program and get discounted admission to any of the Institute-sponsored seminars offered around the country. Discounts are also available to the colorful bimonthly magazine *Naval History*.

The Naval Institute's book-publishing program, begun in 1898 with basic guides to naval practices, has broadened its scope to include books of more general interest. Now the Naval Institute Press publishes about one hundred titles each year, ranging from how-to books on boating and navigation to battle histories, biographies, ship and aircraft guides, and novels. Institute members receive significant discounts on the Press's more than eight hundred books in print.

Full-time students are eligible for special half-price membership rates. Life memberships are also available.

For a free catalog describing Naval Institute Press books currently available, and for further information about joining the U.S. Naval Institute, please write to:

Customer Service
U.S. Naval Institute
291 Wood Road
Annapolis, MD 21402-5034

Telephone: (800) 233-8764
Fax: (410) 269-7940
Web address: www.navalinstitute.org